HISTORY OF CAVALRY I

1914-1919

BY LIEUTENANT J. B. BICKERSTETH, M.C.
1ST ROYAL DRAGOONS, S.R.

WITH FOREWORD BY
FIELD-MARSHAL SIR DOUGLAS HAIG
K.T., G.C.B., O.M., G.C.V.O., K.C.I.E.
COMMANDER-IN-CHIEF OF THE BRITISH
ARMIES IN FRANCE. DEC., 1915 - APRIL, 1919

THE BAYNARD PRESS (SANDERS
PHILLIPS & CO., LIMITED), 6 & 8
UPPER THAMES STREET, E.C. 4

Printed and bound by Antony Rowe Ltd, Eastbourne

CONTENTS

PHOTOGRAPHS OF GENERALS

LIST OF MAPS

Map to show movements of 3rd Cavalry Division from October 8th—October 20th, 1914.

Position of 3rd Cavalry Division, the early afternoon of October 20th.

Map to show position of the 3rd Cavalry Division on October 21st and subsequent days until it was hurried North on October 31st to fill gap at Hooge.

2

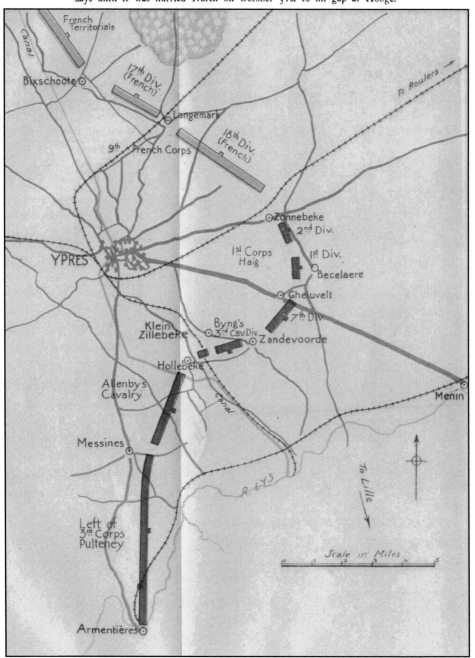

3

Map to illustrate period October 19th—November 17th, 1914.

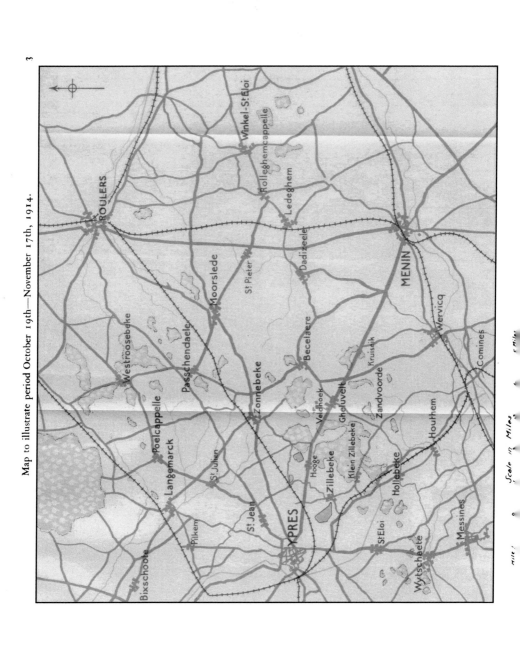

Scale in Miles

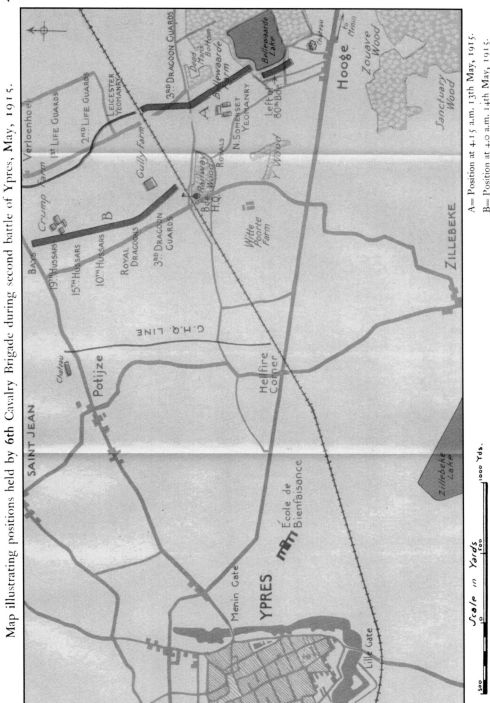

Map illustrating positions held by **6th** Cavalry Brigade during second battle of Ypres, May, 1915.

A = Position at 4.15 a.m. 13th May, 1915.
B = Position at 4.0 a.m. 14th May, 1915.

3RD DRAGOON GUARDS

Dead Man's Bottom

Bellewaarde Lake

Bellewaarde Farm

to Menin

Château

Hooge

Zouave Wood

Sanctuary Wood

Verloenhoe

1ST LIFE GUARDS

2ND LIFE GUARDS

LEICESTER YEOMANRY

A

N. SOMERSET YEOMANRY

Left of 80th Bde

ZILLEBEKE

Crump Farm

Guilly Farm

Railway Wood

ROYALS

Y Wood

Bays

19TH HUSSARS

15TH HUSSARS

B

10TH HUSSARS

ROYAL DRAGOONS

3RD DRAGOON GUARDS

Bde H.Q.

Witte Poorte Farm

C.H.Q. LINE

Château

Potijze

SAINT JEAN

Hellfire Corner

Zillebeke Lake

Menin Gate

YPRES

École de Bienfaisance

Lille Gate

Scale in Yards

500   0   500   1000 Yds.

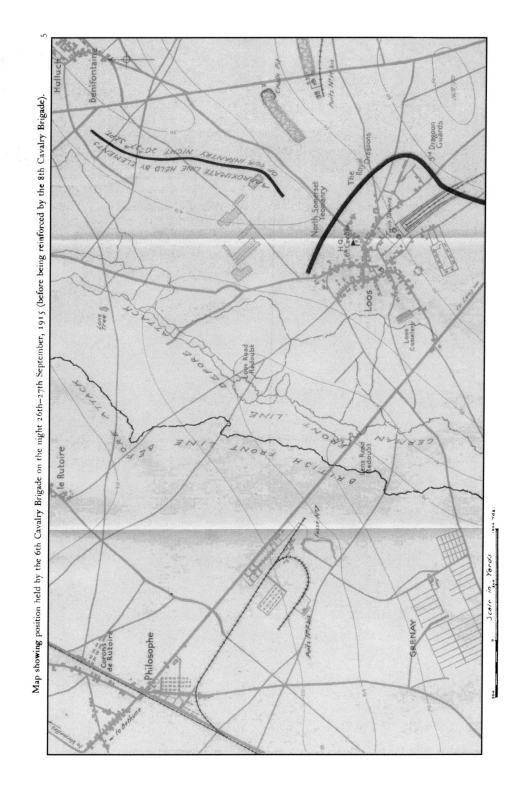

Map showing position held by the 6th Cavalry Brigade on the night 26th–27th September, 1915 (before being reinforced by the 8th Cavalry Brigade).

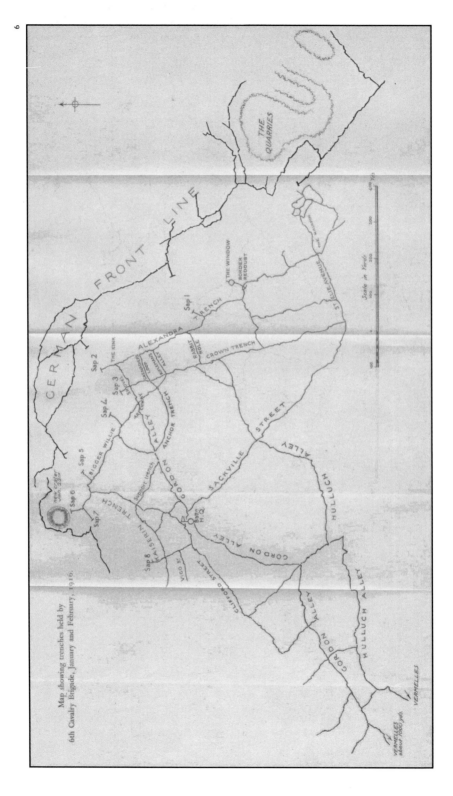

Map showing trenches held by
6th Cavalry Brigade, January and February, 1916.

7

Map showing **position** of 6th Cavalry Brigade, afternoon and evening of April 11th, 1917.

Keeling Copse

Germans digging in

German Troops

MONCHY-LE-PREUX

8th CAVALRY BRIGADE

Point reached by Patrols

Guémappe

Inf. M.G. Sect.

"B" Sqdn. 3rd D.Gs. (2 troops) N.S.Y.

1 Sub Sect. M.G.

Hotchkiss rifle posts.

La Bergère

Details of 112th Inf. Bde.

"A" Sqdn. 3rd D.Gs. in support.

4 guns "C" Batty. (1st pos.)

"C" Sqdn. 5th D.G.

1 Sub Sect. M.G.

3rd D.Gs. H.Q.

les Fosses farm

2 troops N.S.Y.

Captured German Batty. of 4 guns

2 Hotchkiss rifles & 1 Omnes

Wancourt

Orange Hill

Advanced Bde. H.Q.

"C" Batty. 2nd position 2 p.m.

Remainder Brigade

WANCOURT — FEUCHY

Feuchy

Feuchy Chapel

LINE

Airy Corner

Maison Rouge

ARRAS

British
Germans

Scale in Yards
500   1000 Yards

100
90
90
100
110
90
90
100
90
90
90

Map illustrating {
(1) Period in the line December, 1917 and January, 1918 (Vadencourt and Le Verguier).
(2) Area over which "C" Battery R.H.A. fought, March 21st—26th, 1918 (Map 13 illustrates March 26th—April 5th, 1918).
(3) Operations on 3rd October, 1918 (Joncourt and Preselles).

—— Hindenburg Line.   Note.—The Germans retreated to this line in March, 1917. They advanced from it on March 21st, 1918, and were driven back to it in September, 1918. At the end of that month the Hindenburg Line was definitely broken.

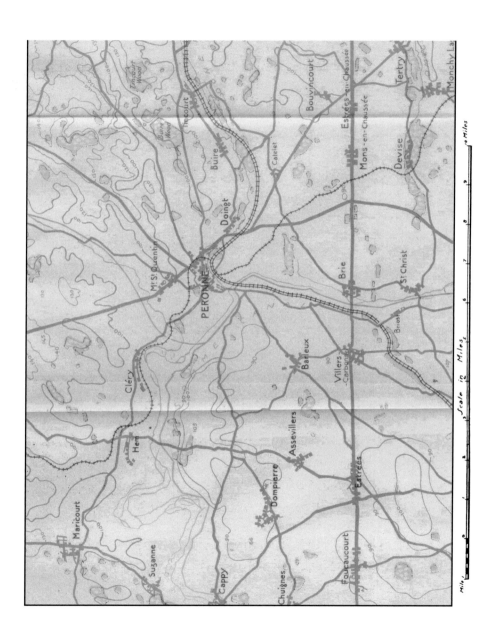

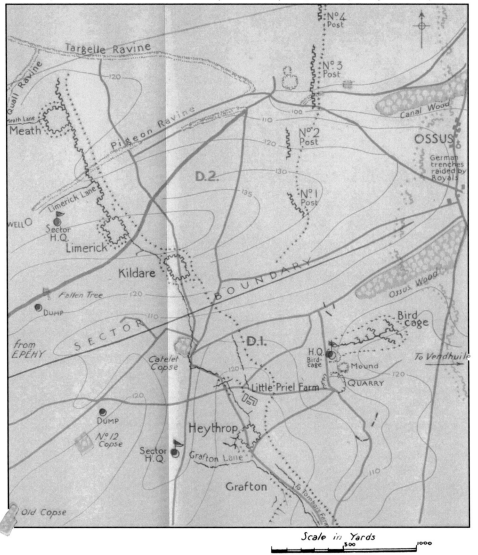

Scale in Yards
500   1000

Map showing area of (1) Operations of 6th Dismounted Brigade, March 21st—27th, 1918. (2) Operations of General Harman's Mounted Detachment, March 23rd—27th, 1918.

Map illustrating the Charge of the Composite Squadron of the 6th Cavalry Brigade near Villeselve.[1][1]

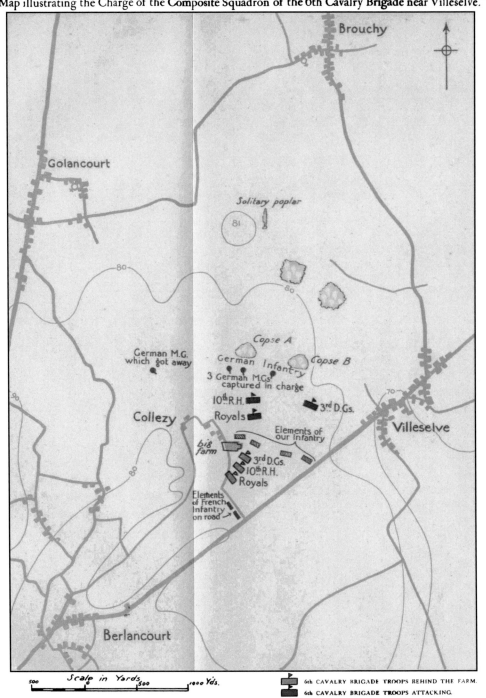

Map illustrating operations of 6th Cavalry Brigade on April 4th and 5th, 1918.

12

Map to illustrate operations of 6th Cavalry Brigade on August 8th—10th, 1918.

= front line morning of August 8th before the attack.
= line on which cavalry were to pass through infantry.
= final objective of cavalry to be exploited East if possible

FRENCH AREA

Scale in Miles

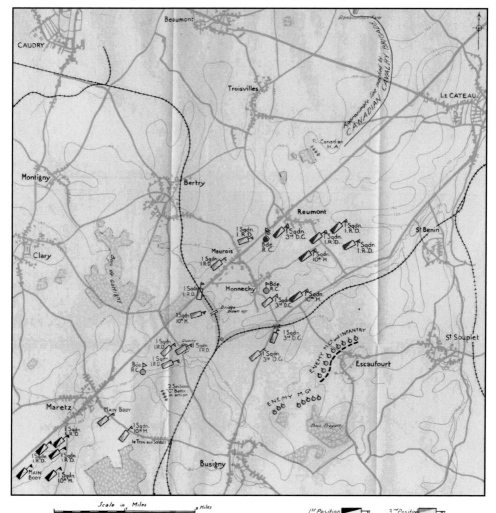

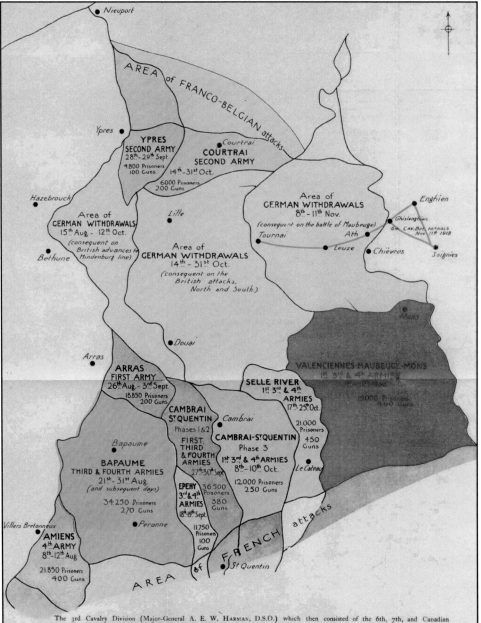

The 3rd Cavalry Division (Major-General A. E. W. Harman, D.S.O.) which then consisted of the 6th, 7th, and Canadian Cavalry Brigades and Divisional Troops took an active part in the breaking up of the original German line on 8th August and following days, and also in the fighting on 9th October.

On 8th August the Division advanced about 12 kilometres during the day and took many prisoners and guns. On 9th October the Division took a number of villages, numerous prisoners and guns, and advanced the line up to the western outskirts of Le Cateau. On the morning of the Armistice, 11th November, 1918, the Division was in pursuit of the enemy between Ghislenghien, Enghien and Soignies.

FOREWORD

*T*HIS *straightforward account of the doings of the 6th Cavalry Brigade, which saw service on the Western Front from the fall of Antwerp to the signing of the Armistice, will appeal not only to those connected with the Brigade, but to all who are interested in the future of Cavalry.*

As a faithful description of the varied nature of work that cavalry were called upon to perform, it should help to dispel any lingering impression that the cavalry soldier had an unduly easy time on the Western Front. By the account it gives of the several actions in which the Brigade did work which only cavalry could have undertaken it emphasises the view, which I myself hold, that cavalry have still a very important part to play in war.

The book shows that from the First Battle of Ypres until the victory on the Sambre the Brigade took part in a long succession of important actions ; and that when it was not engaged in battle its personnel, in addition to maintaining themselves in a high state of efficiency as cavalrymen, were required at different times to carry out most of the duties of infantrymen. It shows also that on occasions such as the brilliant mounted charge at Villeselve in March, 1918, and later in the same battle at Villers Bretonneux when rapidity of movement was of paramount and vital importance, cavalry have a definite advantage over any other arm. The rapid exploitation by the cavalry of the success of our infantry attack on the 8th October south of Cambrai is another case in point.

In writing these few words of comment, therefore, at the opening of this account of the actions of one Cavalry Brigade, I pay tribute to all who saw service as cavalry soldiers in France and Flanders.

D. Haig,

FIELD MARSHAL.

S. Steven

14th march 1920

INTRODUCTION

THIS BOOK is a simple unvarnished narrative of the chief events in the history of the 6th Cavalry Brigade from September, 1914, to March, 1919. A Brigade is too large a formation to allow of the inclusion of personal anecdotes about individual officers and men. These will no doubt find their place in regimental histories. But the 6th Cavalry Brigade, which throughout the war always consisted of three out of the same four regiments, possessed a distinct corporate life.

The Royal Dragoons and the 10th Royal Hussars went to Flanders together in October, 1914. A month later they were joined by the 3rd Dragoon Guards. The North Somerset Yeomanry followed on 13th November, 1914. For a few days all four regiments were in the Brigade together. Then the 10th Royal Hussars were transferred to the 8th Cavalry Brigade, but remained in the 3rd Cavalry Division. From this date for over three years the 6th Cavalry Brigade consisted of the 3rd Dragoon Guards, The Royal Dragoons, and the North Somerset Yeomanry.

In March, 1918, shortly before the German offensive, it was decided to dismount a certain number of Yeomanry regiments and the North Somerset Yeomanry were withdrawn for this purpose. The 10th Royal Hussars returned to the 6th Cavalry Brigade in their place. Three weeks later, when continuous fighting (mounted and dismounted) had caused heavy casualties in the Brigade, the North Somerset Yeomanry came back as re-inforcements. Their regiment was broken up and their officers, N.C.O.s and men were distributed among the 3rd Dragoon Guards, the Royals and the 10th Hussars. The cheerfulness and loyalty with which this order was carried out by all ranks of the North Somerset Yeomanry is worthy of record in the history of a great regiment.

INTRODUCTION

"C" Battery, R.H.A., served with the Brigade throughout the war, as also did the 6th Cavalry Field Ambulance, and with the exception of the first few weeks the 13th Mobile Veterinary Section. The 6th Machine Gun Squadron was formed early in 1916 and remained in the Brigade until both were broken up in March, 1918.

It was felt, therefore, that a short account of the Brigade as a whole would be of interest and value—of interest to those who took part in the events recorded, of value in after years to the more serious historian. Books giving personal reminiscences or individual experiences of the war have been countless. As a true description of what happened they are often inaccurate and misleading. In the following pages no attempt has been made at descriptive writing. Facts stated as accurately as possible speak for themselves. Adjutants and all senior officers concerned have had opportunity of reading this narrative at an earlier stage. My thanks are due to them and to Lieutenant J. F. Houstoun-Boswall for valuable help. The maps have been prepared by me from those used in action. For permission to make use of the original sketches from which Maps 1 and 2 have been coloured I am indebted to Messrs. Thomas Nelson and Sons. If 1918 claims a larger space than other years, this is explained by the complicated character of the fighting during the first five days of the German offensive in March, 1918, when the Brigade was divided up into so many different units, necessitating a separate account of each.

From the earliest days of the war critics of the cavalry have been neither few nor silent. In the minds of a large section of the public there is the conviction that modern war rules out the mounted man and that cavalry warfare as practised, for instance, at the battles of Blenheim, Dresden, or even Rezonville is a thing of the past. Spurs, it is maintained, are as prehistoric as the bow and arrow. Such critics are ready enough to recognise the great achievements of our mounted forces during the retreat to the Marne, the advance to the Aisne, in Palestine, Mesopotamia or elsewhere. But

INTRODUCTION

they are under the impression that at any rate on the Western Front, since the day when trench warfare began, cavalry have done nothing except look after their horses in back areas. It is possible that the bare record of what has been accomplished by a Cavalry Brigade which did not cross the channel till after the battle of the Aisne may help to dispel this mistaken view.

It would be probably true to say that during the war the cavalry-man was on the whole the best trained all-round soldier in the British Army. He could use a bayonet and he could throw bombs. His musketry was of a high standard. He was proficient in the use of his automatic rifle. He had his own machine gun squadrons. On many occasions he took his place in the front line and knew that he was often called upon to do so when the situation was critical. In a word he was capable of performing and constantly did perform all the duties of the infantryman. Between the periods of fighting he was employed on constructing railway tracks, making roads, or digging reserve trench systems. He was lent to this Army and to that to perform whatever task was most needed. He was expected to be ready at short notice to fight as a mounted man, and his training as a cavalryman continued though often under great difficulties. He was taught to ride his horse and to look after it. He knew how to use his sword and was ready for shock action.

. There was a time when the training of " Dragoons " to fight on horseback was judged absurd. But the war has proved the value of trained cavalry who can be used with equal effect as cavalry, as a mobile reserve, or in an emergency as infantry pure and simple. Examples of the employment of cavalry in all these three capacities are to be found in the history of the 6th Cavalry Brigade.

One of the most brilliant purely cavalry exploits of the war stands to the credit of this Brigade. On 24th March, 1918, a composite squadron consisting of one troop each from the 3rd Dragoon Guards, The Royal Dragoons, and the 10th Royal Hussars was ordered to attack a large body of German infantry who, supported by machine guns, were holding a position in the open near the village of Villeselve, a few miles South of Ham. The primary object of the attack was to restore confidence to our infantry who for three days had been retiring before overwhelming forces of the enemy. A secondary object was the extrication of the remnants of two battalions who were almost surrounded at Cugny. The charge was made over six hundred yards of open ground in the face of determined machine gun and rifle fire, both from the front and from the flank. The last two hundred yards was over plough. The enemy far from being demoralised had been taking part in a victorious advance for several days. In spite of these facts the charge met with complete success. As soon as the Germans saw the British cavalry advancing with drawn swords and heard the men cheering, their resistance wavered. Nearly a hundred Germans were sabred, one hundred and seven were taken prisoners, and three machine guns were either captured or destroyed. Our infantry followed up the cavalry immediately and re-occupied the ground which had been lost. The two battalions were able to withdraw and reform.

Other equally brilliant examples of what has been effected by the resolute and skilful handling of cavalry are to be found in the daring capture of Cayeux Wood by the 8th Cavalry Brigade on 8th August, 1918, and in the taking of Montigny, Troisvilles, and other villages by the Canadian Cavalry Brigade in the advance to Le Cateau on 9th October, 1918.

During the war there have been numerous examples of the employment of cavalry as a mobile reserve. Throughout the fighting of October and November, 1914, the 6th Cavalry Brigade was seldom used in any other capacity. Regiments moved up mounted to the threatened point, the horses were sent back, and every available rifle was put into the line.

But perhaps the most outstanding example of the use of cavalry as a mobile reserve occurred on 4th April, 1918. Early

INTRODUCTION

on that morning in the neighbourhood of Villers Bretonneux two brigades of the 14th Division were completely overwhelmed by a heavy German attack. The 6th Cavalry Brigade, two regiments of which had bivouacked the night in the Bois L'Abbé and the third at Fouilloy, was ordered to restore the situation. The three regiments with their machine guns on pack moved up at a fast pace and within a few minutes of leaving their bivouac reached the line they had been ordered to hold. The horses were sent back and our men immediately engaged the enemy with rifles and machine guns. The Germans who till then were coming on unopposed in large numbers were completely held up. Villers Bretonneux was entirely undefended from the North-east until the cavalry arrived. The loss of even a few minutes would have resulted in its capture. Had the Germans gained a firm footing in Villers Bretonneux and in the Bois L'Abbé which crowns the ridge to the West of the village, Amiens would have lain at their feet and the whole course of the war might have been changed. It was a case for mounted troops alone. Lorries carrying infantry could never have lived on the only available roads, which were being heavily shelled, and infantry moving up on foot (with machine gunners carrying their Vickers guns) could not possibly have been in time to save the catastrophe.

It is unnecessary to enlarge on the frequent occasions on which cavalry were entirely separated from their horses and put into the trenches as infantry. Sometimes this occurred at a time of great emergency. It would be impossible, for instance, to over-estimate the value of the magnificent defence put up by the dismounted men of the 6th Cavalry Brigade in the Ypres salient on 13th May, 1915, It was one of the blackest, though one of the most glorious, days in the history of the Brigade. Half buried early in the morning as a result of the terrific bombardment, almost surrounded as the day wore on by hugely superior forces of the enemy, our men beat off every attack and throughout a day of unparalleled strain yielded

INTRODUCTION

not one inch of ground. Again, during the first days of the German offensive in March, 1918, the Brigade fought dismounted for six days in the neighbourhood of Chauny and did invaluable work.

At various intervals, also, throughout the war, the cavalry took over a sector of the front for some weeks. Their organisation and equipment was entirely different from those of the infantry. They therefore evolved their own, and whether on the defensive or offensive were adept in all that pertains to trench warfare. These periods in the trenches and the absence of large numbers of the men on digging parties threw heavy work on those who remained in billets, and it became a matter of great difficulty to keep horses and equipment in good condition. Preparations for mounted operations had sometimes to be made at short notice, when perhaps two thirds of the men had been away from their horses for many weeks. The rapidity with which the Brigade could convert itself from cavalry into infantry or from infantry into cavalry is a proof of the adaptability of the cavalryman to all circumstances.

The experiences of the war prove that trench warfare may very quickly develop into open fighting. It has often been pointed out how far-reaching must have been the effect if, during the latter days of March, 1918, the Germans had possessed several well-trained and well-mounted cavalry divisions. The theory that observation from the air has taken the place of cavalry reconnaissance is denied by none so emphatically as the airman himself. Information of certain kinds can only be obtained by mounted troops.

In a word, however great the scientific developments of the future may be, it is difficult to conceive of conditions of warfare when cavalry reconnaissance will not be needed, when shock action used at the right moment will not produce solid tactical results as well as great moral effect, and when at times of crisis dismounted action by the cavalry will not prove of immeasurable value.

The truth is that in a real emergency cavalry can always be converted into infantry. The reverse is far from being true.

J. B. B.

Brigadier-General E. Makins. C.B., D.S.O.
Commanded the 6ᵗʰ Cavalry Brigade
Sept. 1914 – Nov 1914.

HISTORY OF THE
6TH
CAVALRY BRIGADE

CHAPTER I

FORMATION OF THE BRIGADE

THE history of the Brigade begins with the arrival 1914 of The Royal Dragoons (Lieut.-Colonel F. G. Steele) and the 10th Royal Hussars (Lieut.-Colonel R. W. R. Barnes, D.S.O.) at Ludgershall during the latter part of September, 1914. When the war broke out both regiments were at Potchefstroom in South Africa, where it so happened that they had been training together for two years. The short time spent on Salisbury Plain before the departure for Flanders was fully occupied in completing men, horses and transport to strength. There were a large number of time-serving soldiers in each regiment so that few reservists were required. The 3rd Dragoon Guards nominally formed part of the Brigade, but their sailing from Egypt had been delayed.

Brigadier-General E. Makins, D.S.O., who had recently finished his time as Colonel of The Royal Dragoons, arrived to take over command on 21st September, Major B. D. Fisher (17th Lancers) being Brigade Major and Captain H. Boyd-Rochfort (21st Lancers) Staff Captain. Major Lord C. M. Nairne, M.V.O. (Royals) and Captain J. J. de Knoop (Cheshire Yeomanry) were attached to Brigade Headquarters as French and German interpreters

FORMATION OF THE BRIGADE

respectively.   Lieutenant A. Peyton (11th Hussars) was A.D.C. Captain Corfield (A.S.C.) was Supply Officer and Captain Towson (9th Leinsters) Brigade Transport officer.

Both the Royals and the 10th Hussars had brought their horses with them from South Africa, and there was considerable discussion as to whether they should be exchanged for English horses.   Lord Kitchener sent for General Makins personally and suggested mounting both regiments on horses to be drawn from the Yeomanry. General Makins strongly maintained the South African ponies were well trained and wiry and would quickly come round after the voyage and become acclimatised.   It was finally determined to keep them—a decision which proved to be fully justified, because the South African ponies throughout the war kept their condition far better than English horses.   As however there were not enough South African ponies to mount the regiments when at full strength, deficiencies were made up from the South Wales and South Midland Mounted Brigades.   These horses varied considerably in quality, but on the whole were a sound lot.

On 28th September, H.M. the King inspected the Brigade at Tidworth.   The Royals were mounted on their African ponies, and the 10th Hussars marched past on foot with naked swords, their scabbards having been sent to the armourer to be " dulled."

On 4th October the 6th Signal Troop was formed with Captain W. H. J. St. L. Atkinson (Royals) as Brigade Signalling officer. The 6th Cavalry Field Ambulance, under command of Major W. H. S. Nickerson, V.C., R.A.M.C., had already been formed during September and drew medical equipment a few days before leaving Ludgershall.   Captain H. A. Ronn was the first officer to join the 6th C.F.A.   At a later date he was attached to the 3rd Dragoon Guards and was the only doctor to remain in the Brigade throughout the war.

FORMATION OF THE BRIGADE.

Early on 6th October the Brigade entrained, the Royals at Amesbury and the 10th Hussars at Tidworth. Most of the mobilisation equipment and all the G. S. limbered wagons had only arrived the previous day, and it was a matter of considerable difficulty to get harness fitted and other preparations made in time. The Brigade embarked at Southampton. As the ships had to be filled to their utmost capacity and the embarkation authorities were not concerned about different units but only numbers, the troops were thoroughly mixed up. The headquarters of the 6th Cavalry Brigade were on the S.S. "Algerian" with Lord Hugh Grosvenor's squadron of the 1st Life Guards, while the headquarters of the 7th Cavalry Brigade were with a squadron of the 10th Hussars. The 3rd Cavalry Division filled fourteen transports, which early on the 7th were escorted to Dover, and then to the Downs. Here the convoy waited till dark, when it steamed under an escort of twelve destroyers to Ostend and Zeebrugge, arriving off the coast about 1.0 a.m. on the morning of the 8th. The greatest care had to be taken in crossing the Channel, as the convoy had to pass through an intricate mine field. During the day the Brigade disembarked and camped on the Ostend race course, being joined by headquarters and two squadrons of the Royals, who marched from Zeebrugge (see Map 1 facing page 4).

It is interesting to recall that on 17th May, 1815, the Royals landed at Ostend to take part in the campaign which ended at Waterloo.

3

CHAPTER II.

FIRST BATTLE OF YPRES*

1914 THE 3rd Cavalry Division, which consisted of the 6th and 7th Cavalry Brigades (the latter commanded by Brigadier-General C. T. McM. Kavanagh, C.V.O., C.B., D.S.O., and composed of the 1st and 2nd Life Guards and Blues), was under Major-General Hon. J. H. G. Byng, C.B., M.V.O. On embarkation the division was only five cavalry regiments and one Royal Horse Artillery battery (" K ") strong. Together with the 7th Infantry division under Major-General T. Capper, C.B., D.S.O., it formed the nucleus of the 4th Corps, which was commanded by Major-General Sir H. S. Rawlinson, Bt., C.V.O., C.B.

As soon as it appeared certain that Antwerp could not hold out, it was decided that these two divisions should cover the retirement of the Belgian army through Bruges and Ghent, and then with the Belgians and certain French troops hold the line of the Yser against Von Beseler's army. The 7th Division, which had disembarked at Zeebrugge two days before the 3rd Cavalry Division, was at Ghent on 8th October. Antwerp fell the following day and the Belgian retirement began, the 7th Division acting as rear-guard and the cavalry covering the flank from which an attack might be expected.

On 9th October orders were received to entrain at noon for Ecloo, but this was subsequently cancelled and at 1.30 p.m. the Brigade marched towards Bruges and billeted in villages South-west of the town, Brigade headquarters being at the Hotel Du Cheval Pie in Bruges. The march was long and tedious, as the roads were blocked with retiring Belgian troops and with refugees, motors and traffic of all kinds.

---

*Map 3, facing page 18, shows the area over which the 6th Cavalry Brigade was operating throughout the First Battle of Ypres.

FIRST BATTLE OF YPRES

The 3rd Cavalry Division together with the 7th Infantry 1914 Division came under the orders of Sir John French on the 10th. The following day two armoured cars and one unarmoured car, manned by marines, were temporarily attached to the Brigade. Under command of Captain A. C. Charrington (Royals) they surprised a German cavalry patrol south of Ypres, capturing two officers and three men, who belonged to the 7th Jäger regiment. The nights of the 10th and 11th were spent at Thourout, and the 12th at Roulers, the Royals holding a protective line outside the town. On 13th October the Brigade marched from Roulers to Ypres. On the way an officer's patrol of the 10th Hussars ran into a German patrol on the outskirts of Comines and had one man captured. At Ypres the Brigade watered and fed in the market square, being the first British troops to enter the town, which was at that time untouched by shell fire. Uhlan patrols had visited the place three days before and had looted all the jewellery and wine shops. The Brigade moved on to Gheluvelt for the night, passing on the way Hooge Chateau. The baron and his wife came out and told General Makins what they knew with regard to the movement of German troops. Early the following morning about two miles south of Ypres a Taube flew over the Brigade at a fairly low altitude. The men were ordered to fire. A bullet penetrated the petrol tank and brought the machine down. The pilot and observer, both wearing the Iron Cross, were captured in a neighbouring wood.

Throughout the 14th October the Brigade was in touch with German cavalry on the line Kemmel—Wytschaete and continual skirmishing took place. The Royal Dragoons, who were leading with the armoured cars, drove strong German patrols out of the Eastern edge of Neuve Eglise, while the 2nd Cavalry Division (3rd and 5th Cavalry Brigades), with whom communication had been established at La Clytte, advanced into the village from the West. During the morning a party of seven

1914   Uhlans suddenly crossed the road between the advanced guard squadron and the main body of the Brigade. Captain De Knoop, who was 25 yards away at the time, emptied his revolver at them as they crossed in single file, but failed to hit any. A patrol of 10th Hussars with Captain De Knoop then chased them and accounted for five. It turned out that this patrol had been driven through the brigade column by the squadron of Captain T. W. Pragnell (4th Hussars), who were acting as advance guard to their regiment and had been ordered to push on and occupy, if possible, Kemmel village and Mont Kemmel. The capture by the cavalry of the commanding positions of Mont des Cats, Mont Noir and Mont Kemmel during these days proved of inestimable value in the subsequent fighting round Ypres.

The 5th and 6th Cavalry Brigades bivouacked in Wytschaete for the night. During the afternoon the 6th C.F.A. opened a dressing station in the Cloth Hall at Ypres, but moved to Wytschaete in the evening. The same day the light section 6th C.F.A. was almost captured in Dadizeele by a patrol of Uhlans who suddenly appeared at the far end of the village.

On 15th October the 10th Hussars sent patrols to Hollebeke and Zandvoorde in support of an armoured car reconnaissance, and that night held a line Hollebeke—Houthem. The following morning in a dense cold fog the Brigade again marched North through Ypres to the St. Julien area, and billeted that night on the Zonnebeke—Passchendaele road, the Royals camping inside the outposts of the 22nd Infantry Brigade who were at Zonnebeke. The intention of the 4th Corps Commander was to advance on the morning of the 18th and seize Menin with the idea of using it as a pivot to make a flank attack against Courtrai and the line of the Scheldt. On the 17th and 18th the Brigade sent forward squadrons towards the Menin—Roulers road, and these at once came in touch with the enemy, being continually engaged with strong Uhlan

6

patrols. The night of the 17th was spent at Zonnebeke and the 1914 18th at Passchendaele. Every precaution against surprise was taken, roads being strongly picketed and standing patrols sent out. At that time the line from the right of the Belgians as far as Menin was held by the 7th Infantry and 3rd Cavalry Divisions alone. Had the enemy broken through about Menin, not only the 4th Corps but also the French and Belgian forces to the North would have been cut off and the sea-coast towns must have been captured.

On 19th October " C " Battery R.H.A. (Major J. W. F. Lamont), which had landed at Zeebrugge on 8th October, joined the Brigade, and early that morning marched with the 10th Hussars to Moorslede, where the Royals had billeted the night before.

October 19th was a critical day, during which the Brigade was continuously fighting. Its *rôle* was (1) to protect the left flank of the 7th Division in the event of its attacking Menin; (2) to reconnoitre towards Winkel-St. Eloi (see Map 3 facing page 18). The 10th Hussars were on the right in touch with the infantry, and the Royals on the left of the 10th Hussars. It became clear that we were opposed by large forces of the enemy, and it was not found possible to develop the attack of the 7th Division. Moreover, the 7th Cavalry Brigade on the left had not been able to reach the Roulers—Menin road, and was ordered to fall back on the high ground North of Moorslede. This left the 6th Cavalry Brigade in a somewhat isolated position, and the Royals and 10th Hussars who had advanced from St. Pieter and captured Ledeghem were compelled to withdraw to the West of the village. Owing to the skilful manner in which this retirement was carried out our casualties were very small, although the German cyclist battalions, who were attacking Ledeghem, were well trained, being extremely quick and excellent shots. The Brigade finally gained touch with the Queen's (Royal West Surrey Regiment). Thus " The Tangier Horse " and

7

1914 "The Tangier Foot" joined hands once again in action.* Through-out this operation " C " Battery gave valuable support from a position two miles South-east of Moorslede. The enemy, using an infantry brigade supported by several batteries, now launched a determined attack on Rolleghem Cappelle, and succeeded in working round on the left flank. The Brigade was obliged to withdraw South-east of Moorslede, and finally took up a position on the left rear in touch with a French cavalry division, and covering the 7th Cavalry Brigade as it moved back from Moorslede. Lieutenant J. H. Leckie and Lieutenant H. E. F. de Trafford (Royals) were wounded and ten men were killed. That night the Brigade billeted at Poelcappelle. French Territorials were digging themselves in on the Passchendaele Ridge.

Meanwhile, the 1st Corps had detrained at St. Omer and marched to Hazebrouck, coming into position on the left of the 4th Corps by the 20th October.

At 4.30 a.m. on 20th, the Brigade entrenched a position with commandeered tools West of the Westroosebeke—Passchendaele road. The horses were some distance to the rear in hollows. The enemy attacked at 8 a.m. The position, which was well covered by " C " Battery, was held till noon, when the Brigade began to fall back towards Pilkem owing to the retirement of the 7th Dragoons (French) from Westroosebeke, which began about 11.30 a.m., leaving the left flank in the air. Captain A. C. Charrington (Royals) was killed. During the afternoon fighting began afresh by the enemy deploying an infantry column on Poelcappelle. That night the Brigade which bivouacked near the Pilkem—Langemarck

---

* In the reign of Charles II. the acquisition of Tangiers as part of the dowry of Catherine of Braganza led to the formation of " The Tangier Horse " and " The Tangier Foot " for the protection of that place. On its return home the former became " The Royal Regiment of Dragoons " and the latter " The 2nd or Queen's Regiment." These two regiments, therefore, may justly claim to be among the very earliest of our regular standing army.

8

FIRST BATTLE OF YPRES

road stood to arms owing to a night attack on Langemarck, which was repulsed.

The first battle of Ypres may be said to have started on 20th October, and the three weeks which follow constitute one of the most critical periods of the whole war on the Western Front. Only at two other periods, namely, during the retreat to the Marne in the previous August and during the opening stages of the great German offensive of 21st March, 1918, was the situation equally serious. The enemy were now to waste tens of thousands of lives in a fruitless attempt to win the Channel ports, which they could have captured in September without firing a shot. It has been pointed out* that there were four main avenues of attack : (1) against the Belgians and French on the Yser, (2) against Haig's 1st Corps, Rawlinson's 4th Corps (7th Division and 3rd Cavalry Division), Allenby's Cavalry Corps (1st and 2nd Cavalry Divisions) and Pulteney's 3rd Corps, holding the line from Ypres to Armentières in that order, (3) against Smith-Dorrien's 2nd Corps round La Bassée, (4) against Maud'huy's 10th Army stretching from Vermelles to Albert. The so-called first battle of Ypres was fought on a front which extended roughly from Bixschoote to Armentières (see Map 2 facing page 10).

Having drawn rations at Ypres during the morning of 21st October, and offsaddled there for a short time, the Brigade was ordered about midday to fill a gap at the two canal crossings near Hollebeke between the right of the 7th Division and the left of Gough's 2nd Cavalry Division. The 4th Hussars under Lieut.-Colonel P. Howell were found holding one of these crossings. This position was occupied till 7 p.m., when orders were received to take over trenches from the Scots Guards at Zandvoorde. This was the first occasion on which the Brigade had been definitely separated from its horses. The trenches of the Scots Guards had been well

---

* Nelson's History of the War.—JOHN BUCHAN.

1914   dug (for those days) and were deep and narrow, but the line held by the Brigade (650 rifles strong) was longer than that held by the Guards. It extended from Zandvoorde village to the canal East of Hollebeke chateau, the chateau itself being occupied by the Germans. Brigade headquarters arrived at Zandvoorde at 8 p.m. in the pitch dark and the relief was complete by 11.0 p.m. That day Captain R. F. Glyn (Royals) joined the Brigade as transport officer.

At 7.0 a.m. on 22nd October the Germans began shelling Zandvoorde and Brigade headquarters, and the led horses were removed to the outskirts of the village. Hollebeke chateau was shelled by " C " Battery in conjunction with Commander Sampson's naval gun. " C " Squadron of the Royals, which had been withdrawn from the line for the purpose, then occupied the chateau, meeting with little opposition. About this time a German wireless was intercepted. This wireless, which ordered an attack on Zandvoorde, made it clear that the enemy on this sector had been reinforced by four entirely fresh Corps (which were afterwards proved to be the 21st, 22nd, 26th and 27th Reserve Corps). The Brigade was reinforced by a double Company of the Kings, while two infantry battalions were held in readiness. The day passed fairly quietly, but there was heavy firing at 8 p.m., and again at midnight when the enemy attempted to attack but was easily repulsed. Lieut.-Colonel R. W. R. Barnes, D.S.O., Major Hon. C. B. O. Mitford and Captain G. C. Stewart (10th Hussars), and Lieutenant Talbot (" C " Battery) were wounded. Three men were killed and ten wounded. The Royals were relieved at 9.0 a.m. on the 23rd by the 7th Cavalry Brigade, but the 10th Hussars, who were in full view of the enemy, could not be withdrawn till the evening.

On the 24th two motor ambulances were attached to the 6th C.F.A. for the first time, and were used in spite of the roads, which were very bad, to evacuate wounded to Ypres.

FIRST BATTLE OF YPRES

The Brigade bivouacked at Kleinzillebeke till the 25th, when at 5.30 p.m. it took over the same trenches at Zandvoorde from the 7th Cavalry Brigade. That day the 3rd Cavalry Division came under orders of the Cavalry Corps (Major-General E. H. H. Allenby, C.B.). At 8 p.m. the enemy (strength about 500) attacked and were repulsed. About midday on the 26th, General Makins was informed by General Byng that the 1st Corps, the Cavalry Corps and the 7th Division were to make a general advance about 3 p.m. that afternoon. Owing, however, to the difficulties in which the 7th Division found itself, the advance was suspended. The centre of the 7th Division was driven back and the Gordon Highlanders on the left of the 10th Hussars had their left flank exposed. Early on the 27th, however, the line was rectified by a brigade of the 1st Corps which came up in support. Shelling continued throughout the day, but there were no further attacks. Captain Sir F. S. Rose, Bt., and Lieutenant C. R. Turnor (10th Hussars) were killed and Lieutenant R. H. W. Henderson (Royals) was wounded.

The evening of the 26th has been called the end of the first phase of the first Battle of Ypres. The main feature of the Allied strategy during the previous month had been the intention of turning the German right flank. In face, however, of the overwhelming reinforcements which the Germans threw on to this flank, the plan failed. But the chief result of the severe fighting of this period was that a comparatively firm line had been established by the Allies from Switzerland to the sea-coast.*

At 5 p.m. on the 27th the Brigade, less one squadron and machine gun section of the Royals, who were left in the chateau, was relieved and returned to Kleinzillebeke. On the 28th the first draft of men for the Royals arrived from England. This draft

---

* For an interesting and more or less official account of the First Battle of Ypres from the German point of view read " Die Schlacht an der Yser und bei Ypern im Herbst, 1914" published by the General Headquarter Staff of the German Army. Number 10 in the series " Der Grosse Krieg " (Stalling: Oldenburg).

1914 was called " First Reinforcements," the numbers of which were laid down in regulations and arranged before leaving England.

At 4.30 a.m. on 29th October, the Brigade stood to. Heavy firing was heard and the Germans, who were advancing in great force, succeeded in pushing back the line North of Zandvoorde. Orders were received to assist the 7th Division in a counter attack. The Brigade moved forward in touch with General Lawford's 22nd Brigade (2nd Queens, 2nd Warwicks, 1st Royal Welsh Fusiliers and 1st South Staffords), which was advancing on the line Gheluvelt—Kruseik. The 10th Hussars advanced dismounted through the woods. There was only slight opposition and the line was re-established.

The whole situation on 30th October was extremely critical. It is estimated that at least twelve German Corps opposed the seven Corps of the Allies on the sector Nieuport—La Bassée. If the enemy had penetrated the line at any point North of Hollebeke they would have succeeded in isolating the 1st Corps. It was decided that the line from Gheluvelt to the angle of the canal South of Kleinzillebeke must be held at all costs.

At dawn on the 30th October the 7th Cavalry Brigade were shelled out of their position, and were forced to withdraw from the Zandvoorde ridge towards Kleinzillebeke. The Brigade was ordered out to cover their withdrawal and occupy a line of trenches East of Kleinzillebeke. The 10th Hussars were on the left and the two remaining squadrons of the Royals on their right in support of the 3rd squadron in the chateau of Hollebeke. A strong infantry attack accompanied by heavy shelling developed along the whole front. The squadron in the chateau was very hard pressed. " C " Battery had an excellent target, catching the enemy in the open as they crossed the Zandvoorde ridge. Owing to the loss of the high ground about Hollebeke village the Royals were forced to abandon Hollebeke Chateau and, after repulsing several attacks and taking a heavy toll of the enemy, withdrew

Northwards with their right on the railway and their left connecting 1914 with the remainder of the Brigade, who in spite of continued attacks held on to its trenches. The 3rd Hussars and Royal Scots Greys came up in support. The 3rd Hussars were employed on the North of the Zillebeke—Zandvoorde road in support of the left of the 7th Cavalry Brigade. The Greys were not used. At 7 p.m. two battalions of the 4th Guards Brigade arrived and began to take over the trenches. The relief was completed by 2.30 a.m., and the Brigade bivouacked on the Southern outskirts of Zillebeke. A message was received from the Commander-in-Chief, congratulating the Brigade on the great fight it had put up all day in the face of enormous odds.

During this action Lord Charles M. Nairne (Royals), Captain Kinkead, R.A.M.C. (attached 10th Hussars) and 2nd-Lieutenant Burn (Royals) were killed. Lieutenant A. Peyton (A.D.C.), Major B. E. P. Leighton, Lieutenant C. G. W. Swire and Lieutenant H. M. P. Hewett (Royals), Major C. W. H. Crichton, Captains the Hon. H. Baring, E. A. Fielden and G. C. Stewart (10th Hussars) were wounded. Captain H. Jump (Royals) was missing. He was so severely wounded it was found impossible to move him from Hollebeke Chateau and he was captured.* Twelve men were killed, 37 wounded, 3 wounded and missing, and 4 missing.

The real crisis came on 31st October.

Gheluvelt was heavily shelled early in the morning, and about 10.30 a.m. the enemy covered by artillery made a strong attack against the 1st Division (North of the Ypres—Menin road), who suffered severe casualties and were driven back. This exposed the left flank of the 7th Division. Allenby, whose dismounted cavalry with a few Indian reinforcements held the line from Kleinzillebeke to South of Messines, was also in great difficulties. At 7.30 a.m.

---

* During the period of so-called " reprisals," Captain Jump (Royals), who belonged to a regiment of which the German Emperor had been Colonel-in-chief up to the outbreak of war, was singled out for particularly severe treatment.

1914 that morning the Brigade marched to a rendezvous in the woods half a mile South of Hooge and came under the orders of Sir Douglas Haig (G.O.C. 1st Corps). At 1 p.m. the Brigade entrenched a position East of Hooge, as a report was received that the infantry in front were retiring, and it was hoped to form a line behind which they could rally. The situation could hardly have been more serious and Field-Marshal Sir John French (as he then was) has since stated that it seemed to him at that moment as if the last barrier between the Germans and the sea-coast had been broken down. But the 1st Division, who had fought magnificently in the face of great odds, rallied, and at 3 p.m. orders were received by the 6th Cavalry Brigade to support the left of the 2nd Infantry Brigade in the woods, South-east of Hooge. The Royals and two squadrons of the 10th Hussars advanced dismounted through the woods with fixed bayonets. A large number of Germans were killed or wounded, and the attack proved a complete success both here and along the whole sector.

"C" Battery gave valuable support throughout these operations. One gun was pulled by its crew right into the woods and came into action against a small shooting lodge where the enemy had concealed some machine guns. These were effectually silenced.

The 6th C.F.A. had a dressing station near the H. in Halte (afterwards known as Hell Fire Corner) on the Ypres—Hooge road, and though heavily shelled were fortunate in having very few casualties.

About noon on the 1st November, orders were received to march to the road junction on the Hooge—Kleinzillebeke road and support the 2nd Infantry Brigade, who were being hard pressed. One dismounted squadron of the 10th Hussars supported the left of the line and two squadrons of the Royals filled a gap on the right caused by the Irish Guards being forced to fall back.

Captain W. O. Gibbs (10th Hussars) and Lieutenant G. Pitt-Rivers (Royals) were wounded, 2 men were killed and 9 wounded.

FIRST BATTLE OF YPRES

During this and the three following days the Brigade was used as a mounted mobile reserve, being constantly called upon both by night and day to turn out in support of some part of the line which was threatened. It remained in rear of Lord Cavan's 4th Guards Brigade (2nd Batt. Grenadier Guards, 2nd Batt. Coldstream Guards, 3rd Batt. Coldstream Guards, 1st Batt. Irish Guards) throughout 2nd November. Lieut.-Colonel R. W. R. Barnes, D.S.O. (10th Hussars), was again wounded that day. Throughout the 3rd November Ypres was heavily shelled, and the town was then practically deserted by all civilians except the few who continued to inhabit the cellars.

On 4th November, at 6.30 p.m., the 3rd Dragoon Guards (Lieut.-Colonel O. B. B. Smith-Bingham, D.S.O.) marched in from Cassel and joined the Brigade (strength, 28 officers, 530 N.C.O.s and men, and 597 horses). Ninety-five remounts and a draft for the 10th Hussars also arrived.

On the evening of the 5th the Brigade (1,200 rifles and 5 machine guns) took over the trenches of the 3rd Infantry Brigade in the woods half a mile South of Veldhoek. The finding of this number of rifles taxed the resources of the Brigade to its utmost capacity. But it was imperative that the men should be provided, though it entailed leaving one man to look after fifteen to twenty horses. The relief was completed by 9.30 p.m., the 3rd Dragoon Guards and 10th Hussars being in the firing line, the Royals in reserve. "C" Battery, all led horses and transport were in a farm some three kilometres behind, but one gun of the battery was taken up immediately behind the front line to drive enemy snipers from some houses. This gun fired at dawn at 250 yards range and did good execution. That night about 10.30 p.m. a fire broke out in a barn close to Brigade headquarters, and the whole building was burnt to the ground. Five men were killed and 8 injured.

During the afternoon there was considerable hostile shelling, but no attacks followed. The 3rd Dragoon Guards were rein-

1914 forced by two troops of the Royals and one machine gun. At 11 p.m. the Brigade was relieved by three battalions of the 9th Infantry Brigade, and returned to the horses. The casualties were Captain J. F. Hodgkinson (died of wounds) and Major E. R. A. Shearman (10th Hussars), Captain G. R. Kevill-Davies and Lieutenant H. R. Talbot (3rd Dragoon Guards) wounded. Twenty men killed and 45 wounded.

On 7th November, General Makins was forced to proceed to Boulogne owing to sickness. He had been very unwell for some time, and it was only the critical nature of the fighting which determined him to stay as long as possible. Lieut.-Colonel O. B. B. Smith-Bingham, D.S.O. (3rd Dragoon Guards), took over temporary command of the Brigade. During the day the Brigade again moved up in support of Lord Cavan, and bivouacked at a farm North-east of " Halte." On the evening of the 8th a dismounted party (220 3rd Dragoon Guards, 300 Royal Dragoons, and 2 machine guns) under Lieut.-Colonel G. Steele (Royals) took over the trenches of the 3rd Infantry Brigade between Zillebeke and Kleinzillebeke. The same day a heavy shell burst close to two ambulances of the 6th C.F.A. at Zillebeke, where a dressing station had been established. Both teams bolted. One was eventually stopped, but the other was last seen galloping straight into the enemy lines, neither horses nor ambulance ever being seen again.

On 9th November, Lieut.-Colonel D. G. M. Campbell (9th Lancers) took over command of the Brigade. Captain R. F. Glyn was appointed A.D.C.

That night Colonel Steele's party was relieved by the 7th Cavalry Brigade. On the 10th November the whole Brigade turned out to support Lord Cavan's line, a party of 300 10th Hussars and 200 Royal Dragoons under Major Shearman subsequently taking over the same trenches from the 7th Cavalry Brigade. Lieutenant S. B. Horn (3rd Dragoon Guards) was wounded.

On the 11th and 12th the 3rd Dragoon Guards again turned

16

Brigadier-General D. G. M. Campbell,
(now Major-General Sir D. G. M. Campbell, K.C.B.)
Commanded the 6ᵗʰ Cavalry Brigade, Nov. 1914 – May 1916,
and afterwards the 21ˢᵗ Division.

out in support of the Guards Brigade, and on relief by a regiment of the 7th Cavalry Brigade, a party of 300 3rd Dragoon Guards and 100 Royal Dragoons, under Colonel Smith-Bingham, relieved Major Shearman's detachment. Sniping was very bad during these two days. Major Hon. W. G. S. Cadogan (10th Hussars), Captain T. P. Dorrington (Royals), Lieutenant H. R. Talbot (3rd Dragoon Guards) and seven men, including R.S.M. King (10th Hussars), were killed. Captain E. W. E. Palmes (10th Hussars) and 36 men were wounded.

At 2 p.m. on 13th November the North Somerset Yeomanry (Lieut.-Colonel G. C. Glyn, D.S.O.) marched in from Dranoutre and joined the Brigade (strength 26 officers, 467 N.C.O.s and men, and 498 horses).

During the 13th and early the following day the enemy shelled the bivouac, two men and 30 horses being killed and six men and 45 horses wounded. The Brigade (less " C " Battery) moved back in consequence to some farms South of Vlamertinghe, Colonel Smith-Bingham's detachment in the trenches having been relieved by the 7th Cavalry Brigade.

On 15th November the Brigade, having marched to Ypres railway station, from where the horses were sent back, found 300 rifles per unit for the trenches : (1) 300 3rd Dragoon Guards and 200 North Somerset Yeomanry under Colonel Smith-Bingham to relieve the 7th Cavalry Brigade in the trenches on the Zillebeke— Kleinzillebeke road, (2) 300 Royal Dragoons and 200 10th Hussars under Colonel Steele to relieve the 2nd Cavalry Brigade on the left of Lord Cavan's line and East of Zillebeke, (3) 100 10th Hussars and 100 North Somerset Yeomanry under Major Shearman in dug-outs in rear of Lord Cavan's headquarters. During the 16th there was desultory sniping but little shell fire. Captain Hon. A. Annesley (10th Hussars) was killed.

At 9.0 a.m. on the 17th November the sector held by Colonel Smith-Bingham's detachment was subjected to heavy and continuous

1914   shell fire, and at 1.0 p.m. an infantry attack developed against his right and centre.   The enemy who belonged to the Prussian Guard advanced with gallantry, coming to within 20 yards of our trenches. But the attack was repulsed with heavy loss to the Germans, " C " Battery's fire being very effective during their retirement. Shortly afterwards these trenches underwent a second bombardment, and at 3.45 p.m. another infantry attack took place, this time against the left of Colonel Smith-Bingham's line, held by " C " Squadron 3rd Dragoon Guards and "B" Squadron North Somerset Yeomanry, who suffered heavily in officers and men.   The fire trenches were reinforced by " B " Squadron 3rd Dragoon Guards and "A" Squadron North Somerset Yeomanry, who came up from support, where their place was taken by two Companies of the Coldstream Guards.   This attack, which proved the most determined of the two and was also made by the Prussian Guard, was likewise repulsed with heavy loss to the enemy.   It was estimated that between 350 and 400 dead Germans lay out in front of the trenches held by the Brigade.   The Prussian Guard advanced so close to our trenches, in front of which there was no wire, that the Field Police could be seen threatening their men and urging them on to the attack.

In the vicinity of the trenches held by " C " Squadron 3rd Dragoon Guards, there was a farm building which the enemy had succeeded in occupying.   Twice it was attacked by " C " Squadron, the attacking party in each case being either killed or wounded.   At the third attempt, which was led by Captain Wright, the farm was captured, Captain Wright himself shooting four Germans with his revolver.   This officer, who was killed shortly afterwards by a shell, was subsequently recommended for the Victoria Cross.

About 12 noon the same day an attack was also delivered against the line held by Colonel Steele's detachment.   The enemy massed under cover of a farm in front of the sector held by the 10th Hussars.

18

FIRST BATTLE OF YPRES

This movement was reported by Lieutenant the Hon. Julian Grenfell (Royals), who had carried out a most daring reconnaissance in front of the German trenches. The attack was repulsed about 1.45 p.m., the enemy losing heavily.

Colonel Smith-Bingham's and Colonel Steele's detachments were relieved by the 7th Cavalry Brigade and by the 1st Battalion Hertfordshire Regiment, T.F., respectively. The casualties were: Captain E. Wright, Lieutenant E. W. Chapman (3rd Dragoon Guards), Captain C. H. Peto, 2nd-Lieutenant R. F. Drake (10th Hussars) and Captain F. Liebert and 2nd-Lieutenant J. S. Davey (North Somerset Yeomanry) were killed. Captain P. D. Stewart (3rd Dragoon Guards), 2nd-Lieutenant W. P. Browne (Royals), Captain S. G. Bates (7th Hussars, Adjutant North Somerset Yeomanry) and 2nd Lieutenant Bailward (North Somerset Yeomanry) were wounded. R.S.M. Stewart (3rd Dragoon Guards) and 40 N.C.O.s and men were killed, 85 N.C.O.s and men were wounded, and three men missing.

That night the Brigade returned to the horses, which were brought up to the Square in Ypres, and then went into bivouac South of Vlamertinghe.

The following day a congratulatory telegram on the behaviour of the Brigade was received from the G.O.C. 1st Corps.

It is clear even from this simple record of events that the Brigade had been almost continuously in action since its arrival in Flanders. Owing to the lack of reserves scarcely a day or night passed, when the Allied line was not in imminent danger. In the face of the immense numerical superiority of the enemy no real rest either for men or horses was possible. Even when the Brigade was withdrawn for a few hours, it always had to be ready to turn out in instant support of whatever troops needed assistance. The mobility afforded by the horses enabled the cavalry to be moved quickly to whatever was the threatened point, when the horses were sent to the rear and the men thrown into the line as infantry.

1914   The work done during these weeks of continuous fighting in the neighbourhood of Ypres forms a record of which the Brigade may well be proud.

On 20th November the Brigade marched into billets South-east of Hazebrouck, Brigade headquarters being at Les Lauriers. The march was made on foot owing to a heavy fall of snow and a hard frost, which made the roads almost impassable. The 3rd Dragoon Guards and North Somerset Yeomanry did not arrive until nearly midnight, while some of the transport only came in next day.

The following Special Order of the Day was issued by Major-General the Hon. J. H. G. Byng, C.B., M.V.O., commanding the 3rd Cavalry Division :—

" In circulating the short diary* of the operations in which the
" Division has taken part, I wish to take the opportunity of conveying
" to all ranks my gratitude and admiration for their conduct.   With
" little or no experience of trench work, exposed to every vagary of
" weather, and under a persistent and concentrated shelling, the
" regimental officers, N.C.O.s and men have undertaken this most
" arduous and demoralising work with a keenness and courage which
" I place on record with the greatest pride.

" With the exception of 30th October, when the Zandvoorde
" trenches, held by the Household Cavalry, and the Chateau de
" Hollebeke, held by a squadron of The Royal Dragoons, were
" attacked by a German army corps, no trench has been lost and no
" ground evacuated.   On eight occasions Brigades were sent in
" support of the line which had been partially penetrated, and on
" nearly every occasion either I or one of the Brigadiers have received
" the thanks and congratulations of the Commander of that zone of
" defence for the gallant behaviour of our troops.

" The 6th Cavalry Brigade may well be proud of their action at
" St. Pieter on 19th October; Kruseik, 26th October; Château de

---

* This diary, with the Special Order of the Day, was published in *The Times* of 16th December, 1914.

FIRST BATTLE OF YPRES

"Hollebeke, 30th October; Hooge Woods, 31st October; and 1914
"Zillebeke trenches on 17th November; while the actions of the
"7th Cavalry Brigade at Oostnieuwkerke, 16th October; Moorslede,
"19th October ; Zonnebeke, 21st October ; Zandvoorde, 26th
"October; Zandvoorde trenches, 30th October; Veldhoek, 2nd
"November; Kleinzillebeke, 6th November, have been the subject
"of official recognition and well-merited praise.

"Each Regiment, Battery, Royal Engineers, and Signal Squadron
"and Administrative and Medical Service has more than maintained
"its historic reputation, and during the last six weeks has added to
"the renown of the British soldier as a magnificent fighter, and it is
"with the utmost confidence in their steadfast courage that I contem-
"plate a continuance of the campaign until our enemy receives his
"final overthrow."

(Signed)   J. BYNG,

Major-General

Commanding 3rd Cavalry Division.

23rd November, 1914.

On arrival in the Hazebrouck area the 10th Royal Hussars, amid general regret, were transferred to the 8th Cavalry Brigade.*

On 23rd November the first allotment of 72 hours' leave to England was sanctioned.

With regard to this period of comparatively open warfare, there are a few points which it is perhaps worth recording. The country over which the fighting took place was very enclosed, and cut up by many dykes. The going was extremely heavy. The

---

* The 8th Cavalry Brigade which now became part of the 3rd Cavalry Division consisted of the Royal Horse Guards, the 10th Royal Hussars, and the Essex Yeomanry. The Leicestershire Yeomanry took the place of the Royal Horse Guards in the 7th Cavalry Brigade.

21

1914 Brigade therefore moved by the roads if it was possible, and generally had one squadron only in advance. Flank protection, if considered necessary, was provided by patrols marching on parallel roads. The country was full of spies and every precaution against surprise at night had to be taken. It was usually dark by the time the Brigade arrived at the village where it was to billet. Telegraph wires and telephone exchanges had to be inspected and, if dangerous, dislocated. Roads were blocked and standing patrols placed some few hundred yards outside the village. A central alarm post was selected, and its whereabouts made known to all ranks. Villages were almost always shelled early in the morning, and a start at dawn avoided many casualties. The supply arrangements worked well. Although rations often arrived in the middle of the night, they never failed to come up. The three motor cyclists attached to Brigade headquarters proved invaluable. Without them communication both to the front and to the rear would have been almost impossible. The casualties during this period were: officers, 16 killed, 26 wounded, 1 missing; other ranks, 104 killed, 305 wounded, 20 missing.

CHAPTER III.

SECOND BATTLE OF YPRES

FROM the 20th November, 1914, to the 23rd April, 1915, during which period the Brigade was first in billets South-east of Hazebrouck, and then (from 28th January onwards) in the Steenbecque—Thiennes—Blaringhem area, there are only a few events which need to be recorded.

On 2nd December H.M. the King, accompanied by the Prince of Wales and Field Marshal Sir John French, inspected the Brigade. The 3rd Cavalry Division lined the Hazebrouck—La Motte road, the King walking between the lines and inspecting the troops.

On 14th December the Brigade turned out mounted and marched to a point about one and a half miles beyond Bailleul on the Locre road. This movement took place in order that the Brigade might be in readiness to support an attack which was to be made North of Armentières. The night was spent at Bailleul, the men being in glass-houses and the horses in the open. After " standing-to " at half-hour's notice on the 15th, the Brigade returned to the Les Lauriers area the following day.

During this month French interpreters were attached to the Brigade for the first time. Of the many, who at one time or another formed part of the Brigade Adjutant De Lambertye served on Brigade Headquarters for almost the whole period of the war. Others who were on the strength of the various units for a considerable time were M. des Logis de la Vigerie, Lacaze, de Blacas, Bonnet, Percy Carter, de St. Mars, Tinant, d'Heursel, Valadon and Blériot.

At 2 p.m. on 3rd February, the Brigade (strength, 3rd Dragoon 1915 Guards 250 rifles, the Royals 250 rifles, North Somerset Yeomanry 250 rifles, 8 machine guns) " embussed " at Steenbecque and travelled to Ypres, arriving in the Grand Place at 9 p.m. Much delay on the road was caused by the transport of the 16th French

23

SECOND BATTLE OF YPRES

Corps which was moving South.   The men were billeted in three streets South of the Grand Place.   At 10 p.m. on the 4th, and during the morning of the 6th, the town was shelled, but there were no casualties.   On 8th February the regiments paraded in Ypres at three-quarter-of-an-hour intervals and marched to the trenches, taking over a sector of 1,200 yards from the 7th Cavalry Brigade one mile South-east of Zillebeke.   Seven squadrons with seven machine guns occupied the front line.   The other three squadrons with one machine gun were in support 150 yards behind the right of the line.   Brigade headquarters were with these supports.   On the left of the Brigade were the 10th Hussars (now with the 8th Cavalry Brigade) and on the right the 28th Division of the 5th Corps.   The reserves were supplied by the 77th French Infantry Regiment, and the supporting artillery was French.

On the 10th the support dug-outs were shelled during the afternoon and bombs were thrown into the Royals' trenches. Signs of sapping were observed opposite The Royal Dragoons and North Somerset Yeomanry.   The trenches, which varied in distance from the enemy by 20 to 250 yards, were in a very wet state.   There was no continuous trench system.   At night enemy snipers appeared to be both in front and behind, and the bringing up of rations to " Cavan's " dug-out was a matter of considerable difficulty.   Enemy trench mortars began to be active, but were effectually silenced by French " 75's."   Snow and rain made the conditions still more unpleasant.   During this period in the line it was often possible to hear military bands playing in the woods behind the enemy's trenches.

On 11th February the Germans shelled Ypres with 6-inch howitzers.   The billets in the town which had quite recently been occupied by the Brigade, were badly hit.   The 1st Life Guards, who were occupying them at the time, unfortunately suffered heavy casualties.

SECOND BATTLE OF YPRES

On the 11th Captain E. L. Gibbs (North Somerset Yeomanry) was killed, but with this exception casualties were extremely light. The Brigade was relieved on the evening of the 13th by the 4th Cavalry Brigade (3rd Hussars, Carabiniers, and Oxfordshire Yeomanry), and returned by bus to the Steenbecque area.

On 11th March the Brigade marched to the vicinity of La Motte, where the 3rd Cavalry Division concentrated. Later in the day the Division, which formed a mobile reserve to the 1st Army during the attack on Neuve Chapelle, moved into billets North and East of Merville. Having " stood-to " saddled up all day on the 12th, the Brigade returned to billets in the Steenbecque area.

" C " Battery remained North of Kemmel village, covering a North Midland Territorial division from the end of March to the beginning of May. On one occasion during this period the Battery was issued with some so-called incendiary shells as an experiment, and was ordered to set Petit Bois alight. The shells were duly fired, but with no result.

On 23rd April began twelve days of continuous marching and counter marching through the country West of Ypres in support of the French and British line, which was in danger of being broken owing to the first use of gas by the enemy.

The Brigade marched that day to Abeele, being much delayed en route by buses which were bringing up the 25th French Corps from St. Pol. On 24th April, after billeting at Eecke, the Brigade marched to Vlamertinghe, where the whole division was concentrated.

The first gas attack took place on the evening of 22nd April and the second attack on the morning of 24th April.

The Brigade spent the night at Boescheppe, and the following day marched North to a point West of Poperinghe, and then to Houtkerque. On the 26th the Brigade remained off-saddled near St. Jans der Biezen, and at 9 p.m. marched to a

1915 point near Poperinghe, where the horses were picketed and a dismounted party marched into huts near Vlamertinghe. On the 27th these huts were shelled and also "A" echelon in Vlamertinghe. At 9 p.m. orders were issued (but subsequently cancelled) for the dismounted party to move to Brielen, a report having been received that the Turcos were retiring in disorder over the pontoons on the Yser canal. The following morning the dismounted party rejoined the horses, and that night the Brigade marched to the St. Jans der Biezen area, where it remained till 2nd May. On 2nd May the Brigade concentrated West of Poperinghe, off-saddled, waited all day, and then moved into the Proven—Watou area. At 5.30 p.m. on 3rd May the Brigade moved to a point 2 miles South-east of Poperinghe, where the horses were picketed, and a dismounted party marched to a field West of Ypres, remaining in reserve till 5 a.m., during which time the British line was being withdrawn from Zonnebeke to conform with the French. On 4th May the whole Brigade returned to the Proven—Watou area.

The same day Captain H. C. L. Howard (16th Lancers) became Brigade Major vice Major B. D. Fisher, D.S.O. (17th Lancers) appointed G.S.O.2, 1st Cavalry Division.

The following afternoon a dismounted party of 500 men went up to Ypres to assist the 5th Corps in making defences East of the town. During this work, which was carried out on the Lille road by night, one man was killed and Lieutenant J. A. Garton (North Somerset Yeomanry) and R.S.M. Shakespeare (North Somerset Yeomanry) were wounded. This party having rejoined early on the morning of 6th May, the Brigade marched back to the Proven—Watou area, and the following day returned to Steenbecque.

At 5.30 a.m. on 9th May, a message was received that the 3rd Cavalry Division had been placed at the disposal of the 2nd Army, and at 12.45 p.m. the Brigade (strength : 850 all ranks, each squadron with three officers) travelled in 34 buses to a point West of Vlamertinghe, from where they marched on foot to the

SECOND BATTLE OF YPRES

huts. The 10th and 11th May were spent in huts. The final 1915
stages of the second battle of Ypres had begun, and the Cavalry, as
often before, were called in at the critical moment.

At 8 p.m. on 12th May, the Brigade moved on foot through
Ypres to the railway crossing 700 yards North-west of Bellewaarde
Farm, and took over from the 80th Infantry Brigade the line of
trenches which ran from Bellewaarde Lake, past Bellewaarde Farm,
to the railway line about 600 yards due North of the farm. On
the right the North Somerset Yeomanry, with 300 rifles, occupied
the line as far as Bellewaarde Lake, the 3rd Dragoon Guards with
311 rifles continuing to the left. The Royals were in support in
dug-outs in Railway Wood, where also was Brigade headquarters.
The 6th C.F.A. established an advanced dressing station in a house
about half-a-mile West of Bellewaarde Farm. The 7th Cavalry
Brigade continued the line Northwards from the railway to
Verlorenhoek (see Map 4 facing page 28).

At 1 a.m. on 13th May, a message was received from the
3rd Cavalry Division that the G.O.C. 5th Corps wished it to be
clearly understood that the line now held by the 1st and 3rd Cavalry
Divisions must be maintained at all costs, and should the enemy
gain a footing at any point in this line, a counter-attack must at
once be made.

The whole position was in a very poor state of defence. Heavy
rain had fallen during the previous twenty-four hours. The men
were wet to the skin and caked with mud. In many places the
trenches were shallow and needed repair. If attempts were made
to deepen them, water appeared. The supply of sandbags had run
out. There were no communication trenches worth speaking of.
The wire was very inadequate and in parts of the sector non-existent.
The support trenches were equally poor. There was no proper
communication between the left of the 3rd Dragoon Guards and
the right of the Leicester Yeomanry. The field of fire was every-
where very limited.

27

SECOND BATTLE OF YPRES

Under these circumstances and in the time available it was impossible to do much, but the greatest efforts were made during the night to improve the trenches, to gain communication·to the flank and generally to strengthen the position.

At 4 a.m. a very heavy bombardment began. The 80th Infantry Brigade was informed by telephone, and artillery support asked for. By 4.45 a.m. the 3rd Cavalry Division headquarters and all headquarters in the rear except the 99th Battalion were cut off from telephonic communication. At 5.15 a.m. the bombardment stopped for half-an-hour and then recommenced. At 7 a.m. a verbal message was received from the 3rd Dragoon Guards that owing to the Brigade on their left being forced back, their position was extremely precarious. Their line, however, never changed. It remained the same throughout the day. The Germans who appeared to have got round to the left rear were engaged by our men who fired over the parados.

General Campbell despatched a staff officer to inform the 80th Infantry Brigade and the 3rd Cavalry Division of the situation, and ordered the Royals to push forward two troops towards the high ground between Railway Wood and the advanced line, with a view to using it as a pivot of manœuvre. The remainder of the Royals took up a covering position with two troops detached to watch the right flank. All these movements, which were carried out in the most gallant manner, took place under a terrific fire.

At 8 a.m. a report was received from the left of the 3rd Dragoon Guards that the enemy attack had been repulsed, but that our casualties had been severe. At 8.35 a.m. the North Somerset Yeomanry reported that after heavy shelling the enemy had attacked along their whole front, that the attack had been repulsed, but that the trenches occupied by the right squadron had been practically destroyed. In the event of a further attack the O.C. 3rd King's Royal Rifles had arranged to carry out an immediate counter attack.

SECOND BATTLE OF YPRES

A message was despatched to the 3rd Cavalry Division saying that the 6th Cavalry Brigade were still holding their original line, but that the Leicesters had been heavily counter-attacked and forced to give a little ground. Reinforcements were required. This message never reached Divisional headquarters, and was repeated at 11 a.m., when the bombardment became less. About noon the Germans were seen collecting in a farm in front of the line and later between this farm and the railway. The artillery were informed.

Shortly after 1 p.m. the Royal Horse Guards arrived, and Lieut.-Colonel Lord Tweedmouth, D.S.O., M.V.O., reconnoitred the ground and consulted with General Campbell about the direction of his counter-attack, which was to be made in conjunction with the whole of the 8th Cavalry Brigade. At 1.20 p.m. The Royal Dragoons were sent to reinforce the North Somerset Yeomanry, and a little later the general situation was explained to the G.S.O.2 of the 3rd Cavalry Division. One Company of the Royal Irish Fusiliers now arrived, and two platoons were sent forward to reinforce the 3rd Dragoon Guards. At 2 p.m. our artillery opened a heavier fire and at 2.30 p.m. the Blues counter-attacked. The objectives were reached, but all trenches had been entirely destroyed by the enemy's bombardment and afforded no cover against the terrific artillery fire which now opened again on the troops in the front line. At 4.25 the other two platoons of the Royal Irish Fusiliers were sent up. At 6.20 p.m. about 85 reinforcements arrived for the Royals. All three officers of this party became casualties on the way up. At 8.45 p.m. the 3rd Dragoon Guards moved up about 40 yards to their left, and the line was held as follows : —3rd Dragoon Guards, 50 North Somerset Yeomanry, 60 Royal Irish Fusiliers, 40 North Somerset Yeomanry, and The Royal Dragoons (in touch with 3rd King's Royal Rifles).

It is impossible to convey any idea of the severity of the bombardment to which the Brigade had been subjected throughout

1915   the day.   The trenches were almost entirely obliterated early in the morning, and numbers of the men were practically buried alive. Though it was quite impossible to consolidate the position or to organise any regular defence in the face of this terrific fire, the Brigade gave no ground.   In spite of desperate casualties small bodies of the men held on to their original position until dark. The enemy were unable to make any substantial advance at all.

The 6th C.F.A. were heavily shelled throughout the day, and it was impossible to evacuate any wounded down the Ypres—Hooge road till after dark.   At 11 p.m. the O.C. 3rd King's Royal Rifles received orders to take over the line from his left to Bellewaarde Lake, the Royal Irish Fusiliers taking over the remainder of the 6th Cavalry Brigade line to the railway.

This relief was completed by 2.30 a.m. on the 14th, and the Brigade occupied a new line which ran in a North-westerly direction from Railway Wood towards the Ypres—Zonnebeke road.   The 3rd Dragoon Guards (160 rifles) were on the right, the Royals (186 rifles) in the centre, and the 10th Hussars (80 rifles) who came under orders of the G.O.C. 6th Cavalry Brigade on the left.   The North Somerset Yeomanry were placed under orders of the 8th Cavalry Brigade.   To the left the line was continued by the 9th Cavalry Brigade.   The trenches now held by the Brigade had been begun by Durham Light Infantry Territorials, who had only had an hour to work on them, and they were therefore shallow, unfinished and unconnected.

The 14th May passed comparatively quietly.   At 7 p.m. the 3rd Dragoon Guards and The Royal Dragoons sent out a series of posts to cover the digging of a more advanced line which was to run about 400 yards beyond the one then occupied.

At 9.30 p.m. relief by the 5th Cavalry Brigade began, and regiments arrived back at Vlamertinghe in the early hours of the 15th May.   Captain R. Houstoun (Royals) took over temporary

SECOND BATTLE OF YPRES

command of the North Somerset Yeomanry, all the senior officers of that regiment having been either killed or wounded. On 16th May 12 officers and 194 other ranks came up to Vlamertinghe as reinforcements and a similar number returned to billets. During the next three days the Brigade formed Nos. 1, 2 and 3 mobile reserve in its turn. Digging parties under Captain G. R. Kevill-Davies (3rd Dragoon Guards) and Captain Hon. C. Annesley (Royals) worked on trenches East of Ypres on two nights. On 21st May the Brigade returned to billets. A few days later reinforcements of officers and men arrived, and the regiments were busy reorganising. The casualties were very severe. The following officers were killed :—

Brigade Headquarters :—Captain W. H. J. St. L. Atkinson (Royals, O.C. 6th Signal Troop). 3rd Dragoon Guards :— Captain T. V. T. T. Neville, Captain E. R. Coles. The Royal Dragoons :—Captain H. M. Lambert, Lieutenant J. H. Leckie, Lieutenant G. K. Bagshawe, 2nd-Lieutenant N. F. Browne. North Somerset Yeomanry :—Major W. R. Campbell, D.S.O. (14th Hussars, attached North Somerset Yeomanry), Captain S. G. Bates (7th Hussars, Adjutant North Somerset Yeomanry), Captain R. E. English.

The following officers were wounded :—

Brigade Headquarters :—Brigadier - General D. G. M. Campbell, Captain R. F. Glyn (Royals), Captain J. J. de Knoop (Cheshire Yeomanry). 3rd Dragoon Guards :—Lieut.-Colonel O. B. B. Smith-Bingham, D.S.O., Captain L. V. Owston, Captain C. G. Leslie, Lieutenant H. A. Grimshaw, Lieutenant J. S. Stewart. The Royal Dragoons :—Lieut.-Colonel G. F. Steele, C.M.G., Major P. E. Hardwick, Captain E. W. T. Miles, Captain Hon. J. H. F. Grenfell, D.S.O., Lieutenant A. W. Waterhouse, Lieutenant W. Williams Wynn, 2nd-Lieutenant A. W. Ackroyd. North Somerset Yeomanry :—Lieut.-Colonel G. C. Glyn, D.S.O., Major H. G. Spencer, Major H. B. Matthews, Major G. Lubbock,

31

1915 Lieutenant G. E. Longrigg, 2nd-Lieutenant B. F. Hogg, 2nd-Lieutenant L. C. Gibbs, 2nd-Lieutenant R. Willis.

Colonel Steele and Captain Grenfell died a few days later in hospital—an irreparable loss to their regiment. Of the N.C.O.s and men 78 were killed, 217 were wounded, and 5 missing.

The Brigade received official thanks for the part it had played in this, the second battle of Ypres. The value of the stand made by the cavalry during the desperate fighting of 13th May can hardly be exaggerated. Once again disaster was staved off by the cavalry who fought on foot and proved as good as the best infantry. Though the fighting may not have been so important from the strategical point of view as the first battle of Ypres, yet the bombardment to which our troops were subjected was far more severe. The preponderance of German artillery and the use of gas made it a time of great strain and anxiety. Though our casualties were heavy, those of the enemy were equally so, and the determined attempts he made to break through the British line were brought to a standstill. The Ypres salient though diminished in size was still held by the Allies.

At 1.0 p.m. on 29th May, the Brigade (strength : 39 officers, 772 rifles, and 7 machine guns) proceeded to Vlamertinghe in 36 buses, and that evening moved up on foot to Ypres, taking over trenches from the 3rd Cavalry Brigade. The 3rd Dragoon Guards were astride the Ypres—Menin road at Hooge, having one squadron to the North and two to the South of the road. On their left were the King's Dragoon Guards. The Royals were on the right of the 3rd Dragoon Guards in Sanctuary Wood, and on the right of the Royals was the 8th Cavalry Brigade. The North Somerset Yeomanry were in support. In the line with the Brigade was a Trench Mortar detachment, armed with an old gas pipe trench mortar. The personnel was found by "C" Battery, R.H.A., and was commanded by Lieutenant E. H. Mann. Brigadier-General C. B. Bulkeley Johnson was in command of the

32

sector, Major A. Burt (3rd Dragoon Guards) commanding the left 1915 sub-sector, which consisted of the 6th Cavalry Brigade and 5th Battalion Yorkshire Regiment. The village of Hooge was surrounded by small gardens with outhouses and hedges. The high grass and undergrowth along the whole sector harboured many snipers. Sanctuary Wood was thick with undergrowth and lay on fairly high ground, while Zouave Wood, which joined it, sloped down gradually towards the North. Early on the morning of 31st May Lieutenant F. B. Katanakis (3rd Dragoon Guards) pushed forward with his troop from the Chateau stables towards the Chateau, from which on his approach several Germans bolted. But owing to the heavy shelling which began about 7.0 a.m. he was forced to withdraw again to the stables. During the day the front line held by the 3rd Dragoon Guards and Royals was almost blown in and the houses on the Western side of Hooge were destroyed. That evening, however, Lieutenant Katanakis again reconnoitred the Chateau and it was occupied at 9.30 p.m. Shortly afterwards the King's Dragoon Guards arrived and began to dig in.

On 1st June Lieut.-Colonel J. A. Bell-Smyth (King's Dragoon Guards) took over command of the left subsector from Major Burt. Hostile shelling was fairly heavy in the morning and afternoon.

Throughout 2nd June the 3rd Dragoon Guards' trenches, especially South of the Ypres—Menin road, were subjected to a severe bombardment. Part of the line had to be temporarily evacuated, but was immediately re-occupied when the shelling stopped. At midday several parties of the enemy attempted to reach our lines, but were mostly killed by rifle and machine gun fire from both sides of Hooge. At 3.30 p.m. the enemy again attacked, this time moving towards the junction of the 3rd Dragoon Guards' and Royals' trenches, but effective fire from machine guns and the trench mortar on the left of the Royals' line

33

1915 brought them to a standstill. The 3rd Dragoon Guards, who had suffered heavy casualties, were relieved that night by the 1st Lincolns, and marched to the ramparts.

The fighting on 2nd June may be considered the last serious attempt of the Germans to break through our defences at Hooge. It was the final stage of the second battle of Ypres.

Nothing worthy of note occurred after this date, and on the night of the 5th-6th June the Brigade was relieved and returned to permanent billets by the evening of the 6th.

The 3rd Dragoon Guards had one officer killed, 2nd-Lieutenant A. C. Clifford, and four wounded, Captain G. R. Kevill-Davies, Captain P. D. Stewart, Lieutenant W. Black, and Lieutenant H. H. Dadson. 2nd-Lieutenant A. Hopkinson (Royals) was wounded, and also Lieutenant R. O'Kelly, R.A.M.C. (attached North Somerset Yeomanry). Of the other ranks, 42 were killed, 115 wounded, and 4 missing, by far the greater proportion belonging to the 3rd Dragoon Guards.

On 6th June Captain H. Boyd-Rochfort (21st Lancers) was appointed Brigade Major 9th Cavalry Brigade, and Captain S. G. Howes (21st Lancers) became Staff Captain of the 6th Cavalry Brigade. About this time Captain R. S. Stancliffe (2nd Life Guards) joined Brigade Headquarters as Brigade Signalling Officer.

On 18th June Lieut.-Colonel M. R. C. Backhouse, D.S.O., assumed command of the North Somerset Yeomanry. Major H. D. McNeile had already taken over command of The Royal Dragoons.

During the two following months the Brigade remained in the Steenbecque—Thiennes—Boesighem area. Large digging parties were sent to Neuve Eglise, Sailly, and Elverdinghe.

At the end of July Major J. F. Lamont (on promotion) handed over command of " C " Battery to Captain R. C. F. Maitland.

Early in August the Brigade moved into the area Febvin-Palfart, Nedonchelle, Estrée Blanche.

SECOND BATTLE OF YPRES

On 13th August a large digging party (23 officers and 631 other ranks) went by motor bus to Armentières and began work on a line which ran from the Faubourg des Jardins to the Lys at Houplines.

On 13th September Captain H. C. L. Howard (16th Lancers) was appointed G.S.O.2 Cavalry Corps, and Captain R. Houstoun (Royals) became Brigade Major of the 6th Cavalry Brigade.

CHAPTER IV.

LOOS

ON 20th September the Brigade left permanent billets to take part in the Loos offensive. The 3rd Cavalry Division (less 7th Cavalry Brigade) came under orders of Sir Douglas Haig (G.O.C. 1st Army) on that day. The Brigade marched during the night to the Bois des Dames and remained there in bivouac till the 25th.

Officers from each unit reconnoitred cavalry tracks on the 23rd.

On the morning of the 25th September the Brigade "stood-to" at 5.30 a.m., and at 8.45 a.m. moved off to Vaudricourt, where it halted in the park of the chateau. Here the first news arrived of the success of the infantry attack, the capture of the first line of German trenches and the taking of Loos. The original attack was made by the 4th Corps (Sir Henry Rawlinson): the 47th Division on the right, the 15th Division in the centre astride the Lens—Bethune road, the 1st Division on the left.

At 11.0 a.m. the Brigade moved off at a fast pace along the cavalry track to Philosophe, situated at the point where the railway cuts the main Lens—Bethune road about 1,000 yards South of Vermelles.

The situation seemed somewhat obscure, and Captain C. E. R. Holroyd-Smith and Lieutenant G. R. B. Harries (3rd Dragoon Guards) were sent on to patrol towards Loos. Captain N. K. Worthington and Lieutenant G. K. Benton (3rd Dragoon Guards) were sent out in the direction of Lone Tree, and Lieutenant Hon. W. H. Cubitt, Lieutenant R. B. Helme (Royals) and Captain A. B. Mitchell (North Somerset Yeomanry) reconnoitred cavalry routes in the event of the Brigade moving forward. Captain Holroyd-Smith's patrol reported that our infantry were engaging the enemy on Hill 70 and had just taken Puits 14 Bis, and Captain

36

Worthington's patrol reported our infantry were held up at Lone
Tree.   They further reported that the Germans seemed to be
surrendering freely, but that the general situation still remained
obscure.   It subsequently appeared that the Highland Brigade of
the 15th Division had succeeded in reaching the outskirts of Cité
St. Auguste, but were unable to hold Hill 70.   The 3rd Cavalry
Division formed the only available reserve at that time.

The Brigade remained where it was for the night.   The horses
were picketed in the open.   Officers and men had some shelter in
a row of artisans' cottages.   During the evening the 21st and 24th
Divisions (who with the Guards Division formed the 11th Corps)
came up to relieve the 1st and 15th Divisions.   Rain fell heavily
all night.

The morning of 26th September was misty and wet, but soon
became fine.   Patrols were again sent out (Lieutenant Hon. W. H.
Cubitt to Bois Hugo and Lieutenant F. B. Katanakis towards the
Quarries).

At 11.30 a.m. the 3rd Dragoon Guards and The Royal
Dragoons (each about 260 rifles strong) were ordered to move
forward dismounted and occupy the old German front line trenches
which ran about 1,500 yards North-west of Loos.   The North
Somerset Yeomanry remained in reserve with the led horses.

The ground between Vermelles and Loos was covered with
all the *débris* of war.   Our dead lay in every direction.   Many
of the men had been shot in the act of running forward and now
lay face downwards, arms outstretched, one leg in the air.   The
wire in front of the German line was found to have been well cut
by our artillery.   The trenches, which were provided with many
excellent dug-outs, were full of equipment, bombs, flares and gas
cylinders.   The smell of gas was still very strong.   Major P. G.
Mason, D.S.O. (3rd Dragoon Guards), was killed while in these
trenches.

1915 The situation on the afternoon of 26th September was extremely critical. The 24th Division, who had made what was at first a successful attack was obliged to give ground, and the 21st Division, finding itself opposed by strong German reinforcements, was also driven back. These two Divisions, who were composed of inexperienced troops, had been called upon to march long distances before being thrown into their first fight. Moreover, they had been a considerable time without rations and fresh water. They now became thoroughly disorganised and began to come back in large numbers. The Chalk Pit North of Hill 70 was lost and also the ground towards Benifontaine and Hulluch. Hill 70 became a salient and our hold on it extremely precarious. It was quite possible that, had the enemy attempted a determined counter-attack, Loos itself might have been retaken. There were no immediate reserves except the 3rd Cavalry Division and the Guards Division (the latter only arrived at Philosophe about 6 p.m. that evening).

It was under these circumstances that at 3 p.m. General Campbell was ordered to occupy Loos with two regiments, as the infantry appeared to be retiring, and it was uncertain whether the place was in our hands or not. The Brigade fixed bayonets and advanced by three long " bounds " down the slope into the village, the 3rd Dragoon Guards on the right, the Royals on the left. The line was shelled as it advanced, but there were no casualties. One shell started up a hare, which was caught on a bayonet by a sergeant. On the way Lieut.-Colonel H. D. McNeile (Royals) collected about 300 Highlanders and other parties of infantry, who returned to Loos and helped in its defence.

On arrival in the village it was found that parties of our infantry still held the South-western and North-western entrances. The Brigade at once took up a position running, roughly, through the Eastern outskirts of the village. At about 5 p.m. 18 Germans came out of a farm opposite the 3rd Dragoon Guards headquarters

and surrendered.   The area round the church was heavily shelled   1915
that evening.

The 6th C.F.A. established an advanced dressing station in
the best of the houses on the Loos road just West of our old front
line, and as soon as it was dark all available motor ambulances were
sent down into Loos to evacuate both cavalry and infantry wounded.

At 11.30 p.m. General Campbell, who had received orders on
no account to vacate Loos, requested General Briggs* to send up
the North Somerset Yeomanry in support, as the force at his disposal
was inadequate, the infantry he had collected being hungry,
exhausted and unfit to fight.

At midnight the North Somerset Yeomanry, who earlier in
the evening had been ordered to occupy trenches about 1,500 yards
East of Le Rutoire, arrived at Loos and took up a position on the
left of the Royals, joining up on their left with the Guards.
" C " Battery was brigaded under orders of the C.R.H.A., 3rd
Cavalry Division, and was in position near Les Brebis to cover a
counter-attack should it succeed in penetrating to Bully Grenay.

At 2.30 a.m. on 27th September, General Briggs arrived with
the 8th Cavalry Brigade and took over command from General
Campbell.   The 6th Cavalry Brigade then occupied a shorter line.
The 3rd Dragoon Guards on the right were in touch with the Blues.
" C " Battery was in position near Fosse 7.   The infantry were
all relieved and sent back.

At 3.45 p.m. on the afternoon of Monday, 27th September,
the bombardment became intense on both sides, and at 4 p.m. the
Guards Division attacked Hill 70, Puits 14 and the Chalk Pits.
The machine guns of the Brigade supported this attack.   After

---

* Some months previously (on 7th May, 1915) General Briggs had taken over com-
mand of the 3rd Cavalry Division from General Byng, who now commanded the
Cavalry Corps in place of General Allenby.   General Allenby commanded the 5th
Corps instead of General Plumer who had taken over the 2nd Army from General
Smith Dorrien.

1915 the attack the Guards dug in in front of Chalk Pit Wood and on the slopes of Hill 70.

Throughout the night, which was very wet and dark, the Brigade continued to improve the defences of the village. Trenches were wired, roads barricaded, and work was begun on a central keep. Every preparation was made in case of a counter-attack, but this did not take place, though there was much wild firing from the enemy lines. At 4.30 a.m. on 28th September, Lieutenant W. O. Berryman (Royals) with three men went out to get the situation from Hill 70 to the Chalk Pits, and on his return was able to give a clear report as to the position of the enemy. Other useful reconnaissances were made by 2nd-Lieutenant A. W. Wingate (Royals) and 2nd-Lieutenant A. B. P. L. Vincent (3rd Dragoon Guards). Much valuable information was thus given to the Guards.

Loos was heavily shelled before midday and in the afternoon.

During the period the Brigade was in the village, German soldiers were constantly found hiding in the cellars. Some had been lying there wounded for two or three days, as was also the case with a few of our own infantry. Loos was a remarkable sight when the Brigade first entered it. German and British dead encumbered the streets. Quantities of R.E. stores and equipment of all sorts were found. The canteens were well stocked, and comfortable dug-outs littered with the belongings of their late owners proved with what haste the village had been vacated. Many of the cellars were connected up by telephone, and until they were all cleared, there can be no doubt that communication was maintained with the enemy by wounded men. One German was actually found, shortly after the arrival of the Brigade, operating a telephone line to the rear.

At 3.45 p.m. on 28th September, the Guards attacked Puits 14 from the Chalk Pits and again the machine guns of the Brigade co-operated. That night rain fell in torrents. At 11.30 p.m. relief by the infantry began, and early on 29th September the regiments marched back to the horses, which were just North of

Mazingarbe. The same day the Brigade moved back to the Bois 1915
des Dames, where it remained in bivouac till 3rd October.
The garrisoning of Loos and the taking over the line East
of that place by the 6th Cavalry Brigade and later by the rest of
the 3rd Cavalry Division, undoubtedly saved what was a dangerous
situation. The 15th Division, thoroughly tired out, had been withdrawn from the line and after the retirement of the 24th and 21st
Divisions the Germans would have found practically no troops to
oppose them, if they had made a resolute counter-attack. The
15th Division was again put back and did magnificently, and the
arrival of the dismounted cavalry steadied the whole line.

The casualties were:—3rd Dragoon Guards: killed, Major
P. G. Mason; wounded, Lieut.-Colonel O. B. B. Smith-Bingham,
Lieutenant F. B. Katanakis, 2nd-Lieutenant W. B. Hathorn; other
ranks: killed 11, wounded 30, missing 5. The Royal Dragoons:
killed, Captain A. H. D. Chapman; other ranks: killed, 2,
wounded 14, missing 1. North Somerset Yeomanry: wounded,
Major W. B. Stewart (Lothian and Border Horse, attached North
Somerset Yeomanry), 2nd-Lieutenants E. A. Green, M. H. Tisdall,
G. Babington, A. G. Little. Captain W. L. C. Kirby (12th Lancers,
Adjutant, North Somerset Yeomanry) was also wounded; other
ranks: wounded 11, missing 1.

From 3rd October to 19th October the Brigade was in the
Ferfay—Cauchy-à-la-Tour—Raimbert area. Captain R. Houstoun
(Royals) was evacuated seriously ill from Ferfay, and Captain W. T.
Hodgson (Royals) was shortly afterwards appointed Brigade-Major.
On 19th October the Brigade moved into the district round Laires,
and two days later went into permanent billets, Brigade headquarters
being at Honinghem, and the regiments round Nedonchelle, Ligny-
les-Aire and Amettes. The Battery was at Laires, the 6th C.F.A.
at Cottes.

During this month Major-General J. Vaughan, C.B., D.S.O.,
assumed command of the 3rd Cavalry Division.

LOOS

1915   At the end of October reinforcements of 2 officers and 100 other ranks arrived for the 3rd Dragoon Guards and The Royal Dragoons, which brought the establishment of each regiment up to 26 officers and 651 other ranks.

During November digging parties were sent to Sercus, Ouderdom and Poperinghe. Captain R. C. F. Maitland, on getting command of a New Army Field Battery, handed over command of " C " Battery to Major A. E. Erskine.

On 17th November the Brigade moved into a new area. Brigade headquarters were at Royon, 3rd Dragoon Guards Offin, Loison, the Royals Créquy, Torcy, North Somerset Yeomanry Hesmond, Lebiez, " C " Battery Sains-les-Fressin, the 6th C.F.A. Fruges.

During December a digging party under Major P. E. Hardwick (Royals) went to Lynde, where work was done on the La Belle Hôtesse. By the end of the month all the various digging parties had returned to billets.

On 20th December the Brigade suffered a very great loss by the death of Lieut.-Colonel H. D. McNeile (Royals), who was accidentally killed by a fall from his horse.

A few days later Lieut.-Colonel F. W. Wormald, D.S.O. (8th Hussars) took over command of The Royal Dragoons.

42

CHAPTER V

THE HOHENZOLLERN REDOUBT

O N 27th December orders were received to form a dis- 1915
mounted Division and to remain in billets on short
notice. The Brigade formed a battalion known as
the 6th Battalion. Each of the three regiments
found a company of 320 all ranks and a machine gun
detachment of 4 guns and 42 all ranks. Battalion headquarters was
55 all ranks, making a total of 1,141 all ranks for the battalion. The
7th and 8th Cavalry Brigades formed the 7th and 8th Battalions, under
Lieut.-Colonel E. H. Brassey, M.V.O., and Lieut.-Colonel
Lord Tweedmouth, D.S.O., M.V.O., respectively, and these with
the 6th formed the 3rd Dismounted Brigade, commanded by
Brigadier-General C. B. Bulkeley-Johnson, D.S.O. The 1st and
2nd Cavalry divisions each found a brigade, and these with the 3rd
formed the dismounted division, under Major-General Sir Philip
W. Chetwode, Bt., D.S.O.

On 3rd January, 1916, the 6th Battalion, under Lieut.-Colonel 1916
A. Burt (3rd Dragoon Guards) entrained at Maresquel at 5.30 a.m.
and left for Fouquereuil, from where it marched into Bethune and
billeted in the Orphanage. On 4th January the Battalion moved
into billets at Sailly-la-Bourse and remained there until 9th January.
During these few days various digging and carrying parties were
found. The North Somerset Yeomanry furnished a complete
company as working party, and were billeted in Noyelles-les-
Vermelles, being attached to the R.E.s. On 8th January the machine
guns, brigaded under Captain J. D. Deane Drummond (Blues), moved
into the line and the following day the 3rd Dismounted Brigade
relieved the 1st Dismounted Brigade in Sector D. The 6th Battalion
was in reserve, the 3rd Dragoon Guards Company being in
Lancashire Trench, the North Somerset Yeomanry Company at
Vermelles, and the Royals Company at Sailly-la-Bourse.

THE HOHENZOLLERN REDOUBT

On 11th January the 6th Battalion relieved the 7th Battalion in the front line (D1 sub-sector) from the Kaiserin to "the Window." The Royal Dragoons, under Captain T. S. Irwin, took over from the 2nd Life Guards on the left, the 3rd Dragoon Guards from the 1st Life Guards on the right. The North Somerset Yeomanry were in support at Junction Keep and Lancashire Trench. The sector held by the Battalion was complicated by numerous saps and craters. The distance separating the two front lines varied from 150 to 40 yards, but in many cases there were not more than 20 to 25 yards between sapheads or from a saphead to a crater. At some points, notably round the Kink, the front line consisted merely of a series of saps. There was much mining and counter-mining. Our front line suffered little from hostile shelling. The chief trouble was from trench mortar and rifle grenade fire, and the saps were so close to each other that bombing attacks by both sides were of frequent occurrence. The whole sector was overlooked by Fosse 8, a long slag heap called the Dump. This Dump had been captured in the attack of 25th September, 1915, but had been retaken by the Germans the following day.

Enemy snipers were active, and the first day a party of North Somerset Yeomanry bombers bombed and destroyed a sniper's post and brought back the sniper's box. Another sniper who was in the habit of lying out behind a dead German was also dealt with.

On the morning of 12th January Captain A. W. Waterhouse (Royals) was killed by one of the few shells that fell into the front line, the same shell killing a sergeant (Sergeant S. W. Futcher, Royals) and a sentry.

Every night much work was done. Patrols and snipers went out, new wire was put up, saps improved, new support trenches begun, communication trenches which were unusually long (it being 2,000 yards back to Vermelles) deepened and revetted, sniper's posts, listening galleries, and machine gun emplacements made.

THE HOHENZOLLERN REDOUBT

When enemy trench mortars became unduly active they were effectively silenced by the accurate shooting of our horse batteries. "C" Battery covered the sector opposite the Hohenzollern Redoubt. A section of guns was put out at Le Rutoire under Lieutenant Chapman, and was able to do some excellent work sniping. Though under direct observation from " the Dump " and shelled by all manner of enemy artillery, these guns escaped untouched for three weeks.

At 8.10 p.m. on the evening of 14th January, our guns and trench mortars, together with rifle and hand grenades, were concentrated on an enemy working party which was in the habit of coming to a point near Sap 3. The enemy tried to bolt from the crater near Sap 2 and many were observed to fall.

The enemy artillery then became very active for 45 minutes. Our batteries were extremely quick in retaliation, only taking 6 seconds from the time they received orders to open fire.

A proportion of our machine guns were in the front line. Those which were in support continually carried out indirect fire on the Dump, Auchy-les-la-Bassée, and other tactical points.

On 15th January the 6th Battalion was relieved by the 2nd Dismounted Battalion, and General Campbell took over command of the 3rd Dismounted Brigade three days later. General Vaughan also relieved General Chetwode.

On 21st January the 6th Battalion went into support.

At 6.5 a.m. on 23rd January, our engineers exploded a mine under the new German trench near Saps 6 and 7. Just before the mine was sprung the enemy were heard working in their mine only a few feet from our mine-head. It is believed that some enemy machine guns were also destroyed. The enemy succeeded in occupying the crater and throughout this period in the trenches, the 6th Battalion who took over the line a few hours later experienced much trouble from this crater, which was only 25 yards from our sapheads. During 24th January we trench-mortared the crater,

45

1916 and at 8.45 p.m. that night an officers' patrol (Captain C. E. R. Holroyd-Smith, 3rd Dragoon Guards) went out from Sap 6, reconnoitred the near edge of the crater, and pulled down several of the loophole plates. A second officers' patrol under Lieutenant J. G. Biggs (North Somerset Yeomanry) entered the crater, found it had been put into a strong state of defence, and brought away some arms and equipment for identification purposes.

At 4 p.m. on 27th January, the Kaiser's birthday, the enemy opened a very heavy bombardment on our front and support lines. It stopped at 5.15 p.m. At 5.20 three hostile bombing parties emerged from the German front line in the vicinity of the Kink. One of these parties consisting of 5 bombers made for Sap 4. Our men who saw them allowed them to come on. The leading German lowered himself into our sap and began to advance down it. On rounding a bend he was killed by revolver fire: the second was also killed on the top of our parapet: two others were killed by rifle fire as they attempted to get back through our wire: the fifth regained his line. Another party of ten Germans advanced towards Sap 3. They were all exterminated by bomb and rifle fire before they reached this sap. Of the third party, the three leading Germans only had emerged from a small sap South of Bill's Bluff, when they were blown up by one of our shells. No more Germans emerged from this sap.

On 28th January the Battalion was relieved. On 1st February General A. A. Kennedy took command of the 3rd Dismounted Brigade from General Campbell, and two days later General Mullens relieved General Vaughan in command of the cavalry line.

On 2nd February the Battalion again took over the same sector of front line, but the situation remained extremely quiet. Numerous patrols were sent out and we gained complete superiority in sniping. On 8th February the 6th Battalion was relieved and returned with the remainder of the 3rd Dismounted Brigade to permanent billets. " C " Battery remained in the line till

46

28th February, and then had a very difficult march back to Sains-
les-Fressin, owing to snow and frost.

Casualties suffered by the Battalion during this period were : —
3rd Dragoon Guards: other ranks, 6 killed, 21 wounded, 1 died of
wounds. The Royal Dragoons: Captain A. W. Waterhouse killed,
Lieutenant R. B. Helme wounded; other ranks, 11 killed,
39 wounded, 5 died of wounds. North Somerset Yeomanry: other
ranks, 3 killed, 15 wounded, 1 died of wounds. Brigade Headquarters: Captain G. Sartorius (6th Cavalry), brigade machine gun
(Royals) became Brigade Major of the 6th Cavalry Brigade.

CHAPTER VI

THE SOMME

1916 ON 29th February the machine gun section (4 guns) was withdrawn from each of the three regiments, and the 6th Machine Gun Squadron was formed as a separate unit for training, discipline and employment in the field.

The advisability of forming Cavalry Machine Gun Squadrons had been under discussion for some time. The infantry had found machine gun companies an advantage in every way. Owing to the development of indirect fire machine gunnery was rapidly becoming a highly complicated and expert business. With regard to the cavalry, there can be no doubt that as far as training and dismounted trench warfare were concerned, the creation of machine gun squadrons was most useful. But in open warfare it was generally found necessary to allot a certain number of guns to each regiment in accordance with the importance of its mission and thus the machine gun squadron was generally broken up before the battle began.

The strength of the Squadron on formation was 7 officers, 213 other ranks, 299 horses, and 12 guns. The officers were Captain G. Sartorius (6th Cavalry) (in command), Lieutenant H. P. Holt, Lieutenant S. B. Horn (3rd Dragoon Guards) Lieutenant J. B. Bickersteth, Lieutenant A. R. Cooper (Royals), Lieutenant M. H. Tisdall, and Lieutenant F. B. Ratcliffe (North Somerset Yeomanry). The Squadron went into billets at Offin.

During the next few weeks the Brigade remained in billets and continued training.

On 1st May the North Somerset Yeomanry and the 6th Machine Gun Squadron marched to Le Touquet, and went under canvas near the golf links. Permission to form this camp

48

had been obtained in order that the regiments of the Brigade in   1916
turn might make use of the sands for drill and shooting.

On 15th May the Brigade marched to St. Riquier and took part in five days of very strenuous divisional training. Cavalry were allowed to ride all over the training area, about six miles square, regardless of crops. The weather was extremely hot.

On 21st May the Brigade, less " C " Battery who remained divisionalised at St. Riquier, returned to permanent billets. Major A. E. Erskine left the Battery at St. Riquier, and Major the Hon. H. R. Scarlett took over command.

On 22nd May Brigadier General D. G. M. Campbell was appointed to command the 21st Division, and the following day Lieut.-Colonel A. E. W. Harman, D.S.O. (Queen's Bays), who had for some time been in command of the 18th Hussars, took over the 6th Cavalry Brigade.

On 24th May the 3rd Dragoon Guards and the 6th Machine Gun Squadron marched to the Le Touquet camp, and a few days later the Royals moved to Fressin and " C " Battery returned from St. Riquier and went into billets at Wambercourt. On 6th June the Royals took over the camp at Le Touquet from the 3rd Dragoon Guards, and on 12th June the Machine Gun Squadron returned from Le Touquet and went into billets at Cavron-St.-Martin. On 17th June Captain Sartorius ceased to command the 6th Machine Gun Squadron, Lieutenant H. P. Holt (3rd Dragoon Guards) temporarily taking over command.

All units of the Brigade were ordered to concentrate in billets by 22nd June.

At 8.15 p.m. on 24th June, the Brigade, marching by night, began a four days' trek by way of Domvaast and St. Leger-le-Domart to the Somme area. The Brigade arrived at Bonnay at 5.0 a.m. on the morning of the 27th, after a very wet march.

The Somme offensive was to have begun on 29th June, but at 5.30 p.m. on 28th June, orders were received that it had been

1916 postponed for 48 hours. On 29th June Captain F. King (4th Hussars) took over command of the 6th Machine Gun Squadron. On 30th June "A" Squadron (Royals), under Captain E. W. T. Miles, moved off to join the 19th Infantry Division as divisional cavalry.

On 1st July the Brigade was saddled up in bivouac at 7.30 a.m. and ready to move immediately. Although the British attack, which extended from Gommecourt in the North to Maricourt in the South, was successful (especially about Fricourt where General Campbell's 21st Division did good work), the initial advance was not such as to warrant the hope of cavalry being used at this stage, and at 12 noon came orders that the Brigade was on two hours' notice, and then that it would not be needed that day. The Brigade remained on short notice at Bonnay till the morning of 4th July, when it moved to the Merélissart—Allery—Wiry area, a trek of 56 kilometres.

On 6th July one officer and 58 other ranks from the dismounted squadrons of each regiment went by rail from Longpré to Méricourt to help clean up the battlefield, under the 15th Corps.

On the afternoon of 8th July the Brigade marched back to Corbie, arriving there in the early hours of 9th July, and the same day moved on into camp at Vaux-sur-Somme.

On 14th July the British attack on the German main second line was launched, and the Brigade stood-to at half-an-hour's notice from 4.0 a.m. Readiness to move at 4 hours' notice was required during the next few days, and on 19th July the Brigade moved to La Neuville.

On 25th July a party of 8 officers and 277 other ranks, under Lieut.-Colonel F. W. Wormald, D.S.O., proceeded to Becourt to work at trenches in the neighbourhood of Contalmaison under the 3rd Corps, and two days later a party of the same strength proceeded to the same place to dig on the Mametz—Contalmaison line. The weather was unusually fine and hot.

Brigadier-General A. E. W. Harman, D.S.O.
(later Major-General A. E. W. Harman, C.B. D.S.O.)
Commanded the 6ᵗʰ Cavalry Brigade. May 1916 – March 1918.
and afterwards the 3ʳᵈ Cavalry Division.

THE SOMME

On 29th July three detachments of 4 guns each from the
6th Machine Gun Squadron rode up to Bécourt (the horses returning
to La Neuville), and the following day went up to Mametz and
Bazentin-le-Petit Woods, where they started to construct strong
points, with orders to garrison them when made. Severe fighting
was in progress round High Wood, and the positions held by all
three detachments were very exposed. Captain King visited all
guns and every effort was made to dig in as quickly as possible
and strengthen the general defence system. At intervals during
the afternoon and evening there was heavy shelling by the Germans,
but fortunately the squadron had few casualties. Captain King
was fortunate in not being killed, as a dump, near which were his
headquarters, received a direct hit and blew up.

On 1st August the Brigade moved West, billeting near Soues,
and on 2nd August went into billets three kilometres North-west
of Abbeville. Two days later, spending one night at Maintenay
and Roussent, the Brigade returned to the Royon area.

On 8th August a party of snipers (1 officer, 9 other ranks) went
to Arras and were attached to the 64th Infantry Brigade
(21st Division) in the line.

On 13th August 4 officers and 180 other ranks proceeded by
lorry to the 2nd Corps area to lay cables, and at the end of the
month were relieved by a party of similar strength.

On 27th August 12 guns of the 6th Machine Gun Squadron
proceeded by lorry to Bouzincourt and were attached to the
2nd Corps. They went into the line three days later. Four guns
(Lieutenant S. B. Horn and Lieutenant G. H. Eaton) took up a
position in Prospect Row overlooking Hamel and Thiepval Wood.
Four guns (Lieutenant J. B. Bickersteth and Lieutenant A. R.
Cooper) were in the front and support lines 200 yards from Thiepval.
The trenches in this sector were under direct enfilade fire from
Schwaben redoubt. These four guns were attached to the
49th Division and took an active part in a general infantry attack

extending from Beaumont-Hamel to the " Wunderwerk." This attack, which was put off three times owing to bad weather, finally took place on 3rd September. All guns in the Squadron co-operated. The barrage which started at 5.10 a.m. was tremendous, but the opposition all along the line was very strong, especially opposite Thiepval, where no substantial advance was made.

On 7th September the 6th Machine Gun Squadron and all working parties concentrated in permanent billets, and three days later the Brigade began another long trek to the Somme area, arriving at La Chaussée on 12th September. Operation orders for the attack of 15th September were issued, and on 14th September the Brigade camped near Bussy, moving the following day to a point just South-west of Bonnay.

On 15th September Tanks were used for the first time. Flers and Martinpuich were taken, and our line was advanced towards Geudicourt, Lesbœufs and Morval. The Brigade stood-to at half-an-hour's notice, but on 16th September moved into bivouac South of Pont Noyelles. For the next three days it rained steadily, and the state of the camp became very bad. During this period the Brigade found a working party of 330 all ranks for work on tracks towards Flers and Geudicourt. On 15th September Captain A. W. Phipps was in charge of a party of 250 men for this purpose, and arrived on Windmill Ridge the moment the attack started. In spite of heavy shelling tracks were constructed as far as Flers. The party had 40 casualties.

On 22nd September the Brigade began a three days' trek North, arriving in the Douriez area on 24th September, and by the middle of October were billeted at Verton, Rang-de-Fliers, St. Josse and Merlimont.

On 2nd October a party of 4 officers and 126 other ranks proceeded to Bouzincourt to work under the Reserve Army, being relieved on 20th October by a similar number. The following day

THE SOMME

"C" Battery marched to Le Ponchel and, coming under orders of 1916 C.R.H.A., 3rd Cavalry Division, moved up to take part in the Ancre offensive. The attack on Beaumont-Hamel and St. Pierre Divion was postponed several times owing to bad weather. At Zero on the day of the offensive, the Battery, which was in position near Mesnil, fired a barrage on the sector attacked by the 18th Division, later switching on to the 63rd Divisional front. At 10 a.m. the Battery moved on to Hamel, but were unable to advance owing to numerous machine gun nests. The following day the Battery took up a position West of Hamel village and remained there for five days, when they were withdrawn from the line, and rejoined the 6th Cavalry Brigade on 24th November, being billeted at Roussent.

On 23rd October Major W. T. Hodgson (Royals) was appointed G.S.O.2, 1st Cavalry Division, and on 28th October Captain S. G. Howes (21st Lancers) became Brigade Major of the 6th Cavalry Brigade.

On 7th November Captain J. Blakiston-Houston (11th Hussars) joined the Brigade as Staff Captain.

About the middle of December "C" Battery marched to Aire, where it joined the 1st Army Artillery School as depot Battery. The Battery was engaged in training New Army officers and men, and also the Portuguese. Great attention was paid to turn-out. The guns were also painted in the then new camouflage colours by a camouflage artist.

The 6th Cavalry Pioneer Battalion, under Lieut.-Colonel M. R. C. Backhouse, D.S.O. (North Somerset Yeomanry) left for Maresquel on 20th December and proceeded from there by rail to Acheux for work under the 13th Corps (strength, 26 officers, 823 other ranks).

On 22nd December the Brigade exchanged its billeting area with the 8th Cavalry Brigade, moving to Maresquel, Aix-en-Issart, Aubin-St.-Vaast and Offin.

THE SOMME

Early in January, 1917, the pioneer battalion moved to Doullens, where they worked at double tracking the railway.

On 30th January 5 officers and 87 other ranks of the 6th Machine Gun Squadron left by lorry for Villers-au-Bois, where they were attached to the 1st Canadian Corps. They went into the line near the Vimy Ridge on 1st February, and remained there throughout that month. Squadron Headquarters were at Cabaret Rouge. Much indirect fire was done and the squadron was constantly co-operating in small raids. Early on the morning of 1st March they took part in an important raid which, after a discharge of a new kind of gas, was carried out by two Canadian battalions. The raid was not a success owing to the Germans being forewarned of the gas, which was not as deadly as had been hoped. The following day this party returned to permanent billets.

On 16th March the 6th Cavalry Pioneer Battalion rejoined the Brigade from Doullens. " C " Battery also returned from Aire. About the same time Lieut.-Colonel G. H. A. Ing, D.S.O. (Queen's Bays), assumed command of the North Somerset Yeomanry.

At the beginning of this month the Germans began their retreat from the Somme—Oise front. The week 12th-19th March saw the taking of Baghdad, the Russian revolution, and the occupation of Bapaume.

On 21st March the Reverend Arthur Helps joined the Brigade as Chaplain and served with it for the next nine months.

On 25th March a working party under Captain U. E. C. Carnegy (3rd Dragoon Guards)—strength, 4 officers, 120 other ranks—went by lorry to Arras, and two days later were reinforced by four more officers and 100 other ranks. This party was occupied in preparing a cavalry track.

CHAPTER VII

ARRAS

O N 5th April the Brigade concentrated in the area 1917 Ecquemicourt—Plumoison, thus allowing divisional headquarters and the 7th Cavalry Brigade to come into close quarters from the West. On 7th April the Brigade moved to Vacquerie and Fortel, and the following day marched by way of Rebreuviette to Fosseux.

The Arras offensive was launched at 5.30 a.m. on 9th April. The attack, which was made by the 3rd and 1st Armies, was on a front of 15 miles from Croisilles South-east of Arras to the Northern foot of the Vimy Ridge. East of Arras the first and second line had been captured by 12 noon, but determined resistance at Observation Ridge delayed the bringing up of our artillery, and this affected our attack on Monchy-le-Preux on the afternoon of 10th April.

The Brigade stood-to at 5.30 a.m. on 9th April, and at 10.30 a.m. marched through Wanquetin to a point near Duisans. "A" Squadron (3rd Dragoon Guards) joined the 8th Cavalry Brigade in order to be sufficiently in advance to prepare crossings over the Wancourt—Feuchy line. At 2.30 p.m. the Brigade moved to the concentration area just West of Arras and at 4.30 p.m., following the 8th Cavalry Brigade, passed through Arras and on to the Cavalry Track, which was marked by flags (light blue and dark blue diagonally) and halted near the Cemetery East of Arras. "A" Squadron (3rd Dragoon Guards) rejoined the Brigade at 8.0 p.m., and at 11.30 the same evening the Brigade moved back to bivouac in the open fields West of Arras. That night the weather, which till then had been fine, broke, and a bitter wind, heavy squalls of sleet and driving snow made conditions very bad.

At 10.30 a.m. on 10th April, the Brigade moved forward through Arras, halting for two hours East of the town.

55

1917 "A" Squadron (3rd Dragoon Guards) had previously gone forward again to prepare four crossings over the Wancourt—Feuchy line. Colonel Burt sent two officers' patrols to get touch with the infantry at La Bergère and Monchy-le-Preux.

At about 3 p.m. the 6th and 8th Cavalry Brigade, with "C" and "G" Batteries moved forward to the valley along which runs the Feuchy—Feuchy Chapel road. Here they came under slight shelling, which caused a few casualties in men and horses. This ground had been won during the previous night. During the afternoon driving snowstorms accompanied by an icy wind, swept across the country at frequent intervals. At 7 p.m., the advance having been postponed owing to the necessity of a fresh attack on Monchy, the Brigade moved back about 2,000 yards and bivouacked for the night. It was found impossible to picquet the horses owing to the mud and shell holes. There was no shelter of any kind, and nothing warm to eat or drink could be made. Most of the night it snowed.

At 5.30 a.m. on 11th April, the 3rd Dragoon Guards, with one sub-section of machine guns and one section of " C " Battery, R.H.A., moved up to a point about 500 yards North-west of Feuchy Chapel. Officers' patrols were continually sent out to keep touch with the infantry at La Bergère and Monchy, and an officer's patrol was also sent to act as permanent liaison with the 8th Cavalry Brigade who were just to the North of the 6th Brigade.

At 8.0 a.m. the 112th Infantry Brigade, with whom Major H. A. Tomkinson (Royals) was acting as liaison officer (till he was wounded) reported La Bergère and Monchy-le-Preux to be clear of the enemy, but the situation was very obscure.

Accordingly, the 6th and 8th Brigades were ordered to advance. At 8.30 a.m. the 3rd Dragoon Guards and the Essex Yeomanry moved forward over the Feuchy trenches parallel to each other. Colonel Burt sent forward " B " Squadron (Captain C. E. R. Holroyd-Smith, M.C.) to seize, with one intermediate bound,

the first objective, which was the ridge South of Monchy. 1917
" C " Squadron (Major G. T. Cliff) followed " B " Squadron
and took up a position on its right, the approximate line then being
from the Southern end of Monchy village to the windmill just West
of La Bergère. The right of " C " Squadron was in touch with
the infantry—about 50 men of the North Lancashire Regiment—at
La Bergère. Both these Squadrons came under heavy shell and
machine gun fire from Guémappe and suffered a good many
casualties, Lieutenant Newton-Deakin being killed. During their
advance the Germans, who were seen digging in on the ridge,
retired. At about 9.30 a.m. "A" Squadron (3rd Dragoon Guards)
took up a position some 300 yards North-east of Les Fosses farm.

Meanwhile the Essex Yeomanry moved forward towards
Monchy from the West, followed by the 10th Hussars who entered
by the road leading round the northern edge of the village. They
came under heavy fire from the North during their advance. These
regiments immediately took up positions to the South-east, East,
and North of Monchy. Thus the line held by the 6th and 8th
Brigades extended from La Bergère in the South to the Northern
extremity of Monchy. It is clear that Monchy was not held by
the infantry, when the cavalry arrived, only scattered parties of the
111th and 112th Brigades being found at isolated points.

During these operations Brigadier-General C. B. Bulkeley-
Johnson, D.S.O. (8th Cavalry Brigade), was killed, and Lieut.-
Colonel P. E. Hardwick, D.S.O. (10th Hussars, formerly second
in command of The Royal Dragoons) was severely wounded.

The remainder of the Brigade, with Brigade headquarters
slightly in advance, had meanwhile moved up to the North-west
slope of the high ground East of Feuchy Chapel.

At 9.15 a.m. General Harman ordered another section of
" C " Battery to reinforce the 3rd Dragoon Guards. As the right
flank of the 3rd Dragoon Guards was exposed and the enemy were
threatening a counter-attack from Guémappe, Colonel Burt sent one

troop with two Hotchkiss rifles to strengthen the infantry at La Bergère.

At 12 noon a 3rd Cavalry Division aeroplane reported that the enemy were entrenching on the line St. Rohart's factory—Keeling Copse—Pelves, and orders were received that the 6th and 8th Brigades were to send their horses back and hold the line they had then reached with Hotchkiss rifles and machine guns.

At 1.30 p.m. General Harman ordered the two sections of " C " Battery to withdraw, as their position, which was very exposed, had been discovered by a hostile aeroplane. " C " Battery, under Major Hon. H. R. Scarlett, then took up a position about a thousand yards East of Feuchy Chapel, and fire was directed on the Bois du Vert and on the road East of La Bergère. Observation was very difficult owing to heavy snow storms. At about 2 p.m. the led horses of the 8th Cavalry Brigade and of the 3rd Dragoon Guards began to come back. Heavy shrapnel fire which followed them up caught "A" Squadron of the Royals and caused considerable casualties both in men and horses.

At 2.30 p.m. Colonel Burt reported that his flanks were very weakly held, and that the enemy were advancing 1,000 yards East of La Bergère. General Harman therefore ordered one squadron of the North Somerset Yeomanry (Major R. A. West) with two sub-sections of machine guns to go forward dismounted and support the right flank of the 3rd Dragoon Guards. This was done, two troops and the machine gun sub-sections taking up a position South of the Cambrai road, where about 25 men of different infantry battalions had been organised into a defence post by a private of the 6th Bedfords.

Meanwhile, the remainder of the Brigade were waiting in the valley just West of Feuchy Chapel. About 5.30 p.m. the enemy began to search this low ground with great accuracy, "A" Squadron of the Royals again suffering casualties.

About 7 p.m. the Royals and details of the 8th Brigade
moved back by the cavalry track to Arras. The cavalry track
was almost impassable owing to the mud, and several horses were so
exhausted that having got thoroughly bogged they could not be
extricated. The remainder of the Brigade followed during the
night, having been relieved South of Monchy by the 12th Division.
The horse ambulances of the 6th C.F.A. went up to Les Fosses Farm
after dark and evacuated both cavalry and infantry wounded. The
whole Brigade bivouacked on the race-course West of Arras. An
icy gale and a blizzard of snow blew all night. There was no shelter
of any kind.

At 10.30 a.m. on 12th April, the Brigade moved back to billets
at Fosseux, and four days later marched into an area just West of
Auxi-le-Chateau.

During these operations good work was done by the 6th Dismounted Company under Captain U. E. C. Carnegy (3rd Dragoon
Guards) which had left Maresquel on 25th March. After four
days' work on the cavalry track from the Rue d'Amiens (in Arras)
to the front line, the party was ordered to begin making a track
immediately North of the Cambrai road. On the morning
of the attack they waited in assembly trenches West of the
cemetery, and as soon as the infantry had gone on completed
the track through the enemy first line system by 2.0 p.m.
The following morning the party followed up the infantry attack
on Orange Hill, and the track was ready as far as that point
by 10.30 a.m. On 13th April they cleared Monchy-le-Preux of
200 wounded belonging to the 8th Brigade. A large party of
bearers from the 6th C.F.A. gave valuable assistance in this work.

The casualties during these operations were :—Brigade Headquarters : other ranks, 3 wounded. 3rd Dragoon Guards : officers,
Lieutenant C. H. Newton-Deakin(killed),2nd-Lieutenants M. V. T.
Mott, D. A. S. F. Cole (wounded), M. H. Dulson (wounded and
missing, since reported killed); other ranks, 18 killed, 75 wounded,

1917   3 missing. The Royal Dragoons: officers, Major H. A. Tomkinson (wounded); other ranks, 2 killed, 28 wounded. North Somerset Yeomanry: officers, Major W. A. Kennard, D.S.O. (13th Hussars: attached North Somerset Yeomanry), Lieutenant S. W. Applegate, M.C., 2nd-Lieutenants K. G. Jenkins, J. H. Hewes (wounded); other ranks, 5 killed, 17 wounded. "C" Battery, R.H.A.: other ranks, 3 killed, 16 wounded. 6th Machine Gun Squadron: officers, Lieutenant A. R. Cooper, 2nd-Lieutenant C. G. Lowden (wounded); other ranks, 3 killed, 4 wounded. The 3rd Dragoon Guards had 190 horses killed.

It would be difficult to conceive of worse weather for important operations. Numbers of men in the Brigade, after having been out in the open for three nights in the snow, had to be evacuated suffering from exposure. The horses suffered even more than the men. Every night they stood out in the driving snow up to their hocks in mud and slush. On one occasion it was impossible to water them for close on 48 hours. It was, however, extraordinary how quickly they picked up after a week's rest and care.

On 19th April the Brigade moved into the Maintenay—Vron— Nempont area. On 23rd April a Gotha machine with compass out of order came down near Vron. The occupants, two officers and one N.C.O., succeeded in partially burning one of the engines before they were taken prisoners by a Royals' exercise party which happened to be passing at the time.

Three hundred riding horses arrived from Boulogne on 30th April, thus making the Brigade up to strength after the losses at Arras. On 5th May the Corps Commander presented medal ribands at Petit Préaux. On 9th May the Brigade held a Horse Show at Petit Préaux.

CHAPTER VIII

EPÉHY AND THE BIRDCAGE

T HE 2nd, 3rd, 4th and 5th Cavalry Divisions having 1917
been ordered to concentrate in the area East and South
of Peronne, the Brigade left billets on 12th May, and
after three days' trek arrived at Bussy-les-Daours.
" C " Battery left the Brigade here and joined the
2nd Cavalry Division.

On 17th May the Brigade moved to Bayonvillers and
Harbonniéres, and next day marched into camp just North of the
village of Buire, 4 miles East of Peronne. The whole of this area
had been evacuated by the Germans in their retreat to the Hindenburg Line two months before. It was a fine, open, undulating
country, almost entirely grass land, and affording wonderful grazing
for the horses. Every village had been systematically destroyed by
the enemy before they retired and all civilians removed. The
Brigade camp was well situated on ground sloping down to the
Cologne river. Officers and men made themselves bivouacs from
material taken from old German dug-outs in the neighbourhood.

On the night of 21st May " C " Battery went into action
near Ronssoy. About this time Lieutenant R. Lakin (Oxfordshire
Hussars) became A.D.C. to General Harman, in place of Lieutenant
S. Ricardo (General List), who was evacuated sick.

On 23rd May the 6th and 7th Cavalry Brigades began to relieve
portions of the 3rd and 5th Cavalry Brigades in Sector D of the
cavalry corps front. The trench line taken over extended from
Tombois Farm (exclusive) in the South to Pigeon Quarry (500 yards
East of the junction of Pigeon and Targelle ravine) in the north.
This front was divided into sub-sectors, D1 and D2 (the boundary
between them being a sunk road North of Catelet Copse), and had
three main lines of defence, the Outpost, Intermediate (Green), and

1917 Second (Brown) lines. The intermediate line eventually consisted of the posts Meath, Limerick, Kildare, Heythrop, Grafton, which were joined up to form a continuous trench system. The Brown line ran East of Epéhy. Sector headquarters was in a railway embankment immediately East of Epéhy.

The Brigade took over D1 sub-sector, and by the morning of the 25th May one-and-a-half squadrons of the Royals were in the Birdcage under Captain H. M. P. Hewett, the 3rd Dragoon Guards in the Intermediate line, the remainder of the Royals in support to the 3rd Dragoon Guards, and the North Somerset Yeomanry in the Second line. Two Vickers guns, subsequently three, were put into the Birdcage, the rest being in the Intermediate line, with two in reserve. Colonel Burt was in command of the sub-sector and General Harman of the sector. The artillery, consisting of " C " and " K " Batteries, two Field Batteries and one Howitzer Battery, were under Lieut.-Colonel A. R. Wainewright, and the machine guns (6th and 7th Machine Gun Squadrons) were in charge of Major F. King.

The whole sector was quiet with the exception of the Birdcage, which was subjected daily to Trench Mortar fire, and Petit Priel farm which was continually shelled. The Birdcage was in a very isolated position and could only be approached by night. The wire was thin and the trenches were shallow and unfinished.

Ossus Wood and the area round the outposts were patrolled almost every night, and work was at once begun on strengthening the Birdcage and improving the Intermediate line.

About 2.0 a.m. on 28th May, the enemy made a raid on the communication trench (about 400 yards long), which ran from the Quarry to the Birdcage. The North Somerset Yeomanry, who had relieved the Royals that night, succeeded in driving off a large party of Germans, but Corporal Dunn (North Somerset Yeomanry), who was on his way down the trench with a broken telephone in his hand, was captured by the raiding party and taken to the German line.

On the evening of 1st June relief by the 8th Cavalry Brigade began and was completed by the morning of the 3rd. Lieut.-Colonel Lord Tweedmouth took over command of D1 sub-sector and General Portal relieved General Harman. During these nine days much work had been done. The Birdcage and its communication trench were wired and greatly improved, and in the Intermediate line all the redoubts were strengthened, new machine gun emplacements made, and dug-outs begun.

The Brigade marched back to camp at Buire and took over duties of Reserve Brigade.

By the morning of 12th June the Brigade had relieved the 7th Cavalry Brigade in D2 sub-sector, General Seymour taking over command of D sector from General Portal the same day. One-and-a-half squadrons of the Royals were in the outpost line, the 3rd Dragoon Guards in the Intermediate line, the remainder of the Royals being in support, and the North Somerset Yeomanry in the Second line. The Machine Gun Squadron had one gun in No. 1 Post and one in No. 3 Post, the rest (except two in reserve) were doing S.O.S. and barrage fire from the Intermediate line. " C " Battery took over " K " Battery's positions near Epéhy, and during the next ten days took part in several raids done by the cavalry, the most notable of which was that done by the Greys on Guillemont Farm and by the Royals on enemy posts between Ossus and Canal Woods.

Much work was done at night. The trenches were widened, deepened and revetted, tactical rays of wire were put out, a new Sub-sector headquarters with " elephant " dug-outs was begun in Pigeon Ravine, and communication trenches from the Barricade to No. 1 Post were started.

Officers' patrols went out every night from one of the outposts. The distance separating our own and the enemy outposts was about 800 yards.

EPÉHY AND THE BIRDCAGE

At 1.30 a.m. on 15th June, an enemy patrol attempted to bomb one of our wiring parties in front of No. 1 Post, but were driven off. Regiments relieved each other every six days in the outpost line.

Our artillery constantly shelled Ossus Wood, Vendhuille and La Terrière, and the machine guns carried out indirect harassing fire on cross roads and other tactical points.

On 21st June the enemy in two parties attempted to raid the Birdcage, occupied at that time by the Leicester Yeomanry: one party was driven off by rapid fire, the other was caught by its own T.M. barrage. Three wounded Germans were brought in and seven dead, including an officer, were left in our wire.

On 22nd June General Harman relieved General Seymour.

Early on the morning of 25th June a raid was carried out on the enemy outposts between Canal Wood and Ossus Wood. The raiding party, which was divided into two, consisted of 100 all ranks, all of whom were Royals except a few men from the 3rd Dragoon Guards and North Somerset Yeomanry who were among the Scouts, and six men from the 3rd Field Squadron who were responsible for the Bangalore torpedoes.

The right party under Lieutenant R. H. W. Henderson (with Lieutenant J. S. Dunville in charge of the advance scouts) attacked South of the road which led from No. 3 Post to Ossus Wood, and the left party under Lieutenant R. B. Helme (with Lieutenant V. C. Rice, North Somerset Yeomanry, in charge of the advance Scouts) attacked to the North of it. Lieutenant J. B. Bickersteth was in charge of the Hotchkiss rifles and covering party.

The march across No Man's Land, a distance of about 750 yards was made on a compass bearing, each party moving separately. Dense thistles as high as a man's head increased the difficulty of keeping direction. A tape was laid in order to assist the return journey. Both parties lay up about 200 yards from the enemy's wire until the barrage started at zero (1.10 a.m.) and then moved forward with the barrage. From the first there was considerable opposition, and each party came under heavy rifle and trench mortar fire. After being delayed some minutes by an extra belt of wire, the right party reached the enemy's main wire. A Bangalore torpedo was put in position, but at first failed to go off, thus causing still further delay. By the time the actual trenches were reached, the scheduled time limit was almost up. Several Germans, however, were killed before the party was forced to withdraw in order to escape our own barrage.

The left party cut the first belt of wire and prepared to blow up the main belt, but found some white posts marking a track into the enemy trenches. They entered by this track. A considerable number of Germans were killed and a machine gun in a shell hole was destroyed. Lieutenant Rice had his arm broken by a bullet, but killed two Germans and carried on till completion of the raid. One prisoner was taken, but died before he could be got in. Several identifications were procured, showing the enemy to belong to the 2nd Battalion 124th Infantry Regiment. Unfortunately, during this raid Lieutenant Helme was killed and Lieutenant Dunville so severely wounded that he died in hospital two days later.

The casualties during this period in the trenches were:— 3rd Dragoon Guards: officers, 2nd-Lieutenant T. P. Brill (wounded) ; other ranks, 2 killed, 7 wounded. The Royal Dragoons : officers, Lieutenant R. B. Helme (killed), 2nd-Lieutenant J. S. Dunville (died of wounds) and 2nd-Lieutenant C. C. H. Hilton-Green (wounded); other ranks, 2 killed, 19 wounded, 2 missing. North Somerset Yeomanry: officers, 2nd-Lieutenant V. C. Rice (wounded); other ranks, 10 wounded, 1 missing.

Second-Lieutenant J. S. Dunville (Royals) was awarded the Victoria Cross for his work during this raid. The official account is as follows :—" For most conspicuous bravery. When " in charge of a party consisting of scouts and Royal Engineers " engaged in the demolition of the enemy's wire, this officer displayed " great gallantry and disregard of all personal danger. In order to

1917 " ensure the absolute success of the work entrusted to him, Second-
" Lieutenant Dunville placed himself between a non-commissioned
" officer of the Royal Engineers and the enemy's fire, and, thus
" protected, this non-commissioned officer was enabled to complete a
" work of great importance. 2nd-Lieutenant Dunville, although
" severely wounded, continued to direct his men in the wire-cutting
" and general operations until the raid was successfully completed,
" thereby setting a magnificent example of courage, determination, and
" devotion to duty to all ranks under his command. This gallant
" officer has since succumbed to his wounds."

The Brigade remained in camp at Buire till 4th July, and then
began a four days' march to Auchel, Marles-les-Mines and
Lapugnoy. The Brigade remained in this district till 16th July,
when it marched into the Haverskerque area. Brigade headquarters were at Les Lauriers, occupying the same house as in
November, 1914. The Brigade area extended along the road from
Le Sart to Haverskerque.

At the end of July the Brigade sent officers and men to Camiers
for Hotchkiss Rifle Training and also to St. Pol for Physical and
Bayonet Training.

On 5th August Captain J. Blakiston-Houston, D.S.O.
(11th Hussars) was appointed D.A.A. and Q.M.G. of the Division,
and a few days later Captain S. C. Deed, M.C. (General List,
10th Hussars) was made Staff Captain of the 6th Brigade.

On 6th August a working party (strength 5 officers and 152
other ranks) proceeded to a point near Vlamertinghe for work under
the 5th Army near St. Jean (East of Ypres). 2nd-Lieutenant F. T.
Turpin (North Somerset Yeomanry) was wounded, and the Royals
had several casualties.

On 12th August all the surplus men of the regiments and the
6th Machine Gun Squadron proceeded to the base.

"C" Battery left the Brigade on 31st August to be attached to the 5th Army as instructional battery near St. Omer, not rejoining until the beginning of November.

During the period at Haverskerque regimental and brigade training took place.

Brigade and Divisional horse shows were also held, and on 1st September there was a Cavalry Corps horse show near St. Pol. On 1st October the 3rd Dragoon Guards held sports, the chief event of which was a three-and-a-half mile race, won from a field of 150 by Lieutenant Vincent (3rd Dragoon Guards).

On 9th October Captain S. C. Deed, M.C. (Staff Captain), and Captain U. E. C. Carnegy, M.C., proceeded to Egypt to take up staff appointments there. Captain R. M. Wootten (6th Inniskilling Dragoons) became Staff Captain of the Brigade.

CHAPTER IX.

VADENCOURT AND TERTRY

O N 19th October the Brigade began a trek of several days, and by 24th October were in billets along the Somme Valley from Abbeville to Longpré.

Three days later a Brigade working party (strength, 9 officers, 350 other ranks) proceeded by lorry to Doingt (East of Peronne) to erect stables and huts, the 3rd Cavalry Pioneer Battalion being under Major G. T. Cliff (3rd Dragoon Guards). Three weeks later the whole of this party rejoined.

On 12th November "C" Battery with remainder of 4th Brigade, R.H.A., marched to Le Mesnil-en-Artois, and on the night of 20th November were in a position South of Havrincourt Wood. They took part in the original barrage for the Cambrai offensive, and remained in position till 30th November.

On 17th November the Brigade marched to the Beaucourt-Contay area and remained in billets till 4 p.m. the following afternoon, when the march was continued by night to Suzanne—the 3rd Dragoon Guards being at Cappy.

General Harman was in command of the Division in the absence of General Vaughan, and Colonel Burt was in temporary command of the Brigade.

At 6 a.m. on Tuesday, 20th November, the attack on the Cambrai salient, which had been in preparation for many weeks, began. The chief features of the offensive were the use of the infantry who were holding the line as the primary attacking force, and the employment of Tanks on a large scale. The enemy were not expecting the attack, which proved a complete surprise. The Hindenburg line was carried, and with the exception of some resistance at Havrincourt, and later at Flesquières (which was after-

68

wards retaken by the enemy), all objectives from Masnières to   1917
Noyelles were taken with few casualties.

The 1st Cavalry Division, which was at Fins when the attack
started, moved forward but were held up at first by the recapture
of Flesquières. They subsequently did most useful work, both
mounted and dismounted. The 5th Cavalry Division supported
the infantry along the L'Escaut canal by Marcoing and Masnières,
one squadron of the Fort Garry Horse succeeding in crossing the
canal. The 2nd Cavalry Division moved up in support of the
5th Cavalry Division, but returned during the night to Villers
Plouich.

The Brigade stood-to at Suzanne from 8.30 a.m. ready to move
at half-an-hour's notice, but later in the day off-saddled. Heavy
rain began during the afternoon and continued persistently for two
days. The following morning the Brigade stood-to at 6.30 a.m.,
but it became evident as the day wore on that a forward movement
was unlikely.

On 23rd November the Brigade moved back to the Talmas—
Contay—Herissart area. The fighting round Cambrai had become
stationary, the enemy having brought up strong reinforcements.
The 1st and 2nd Cavalry Divisions were employed dismounted in
Bourlon Wood.

On 29th November the Brigade was ordered to send a dismounted Battalion to the trenches, the whole Division finding a
Brigade. The advance party with transport left on 30th November
for Templeux-le-Guérard. That morning, however, the Germans
attacked from Bantouzelle to Vendhuille. They took Villers
Guislain, La Vacquerie and Lateau Wood, and were in Gouzeaucourt
before anyone suspected the rapidity of the attack. At 12 noon the
Brigade was ordered to be ready to move mounted at one hour's
notice; the dismounted Battalion being cancelled and transport
ordered to rejoin. " C " Battery went into action under the 24th
Division at Templeux-le-Guérard and remained there till 11th

1917 December. The same evening orders were received to form the Battalion as before, and the following morning the 6th Cavalry Battalion under Lieut.-Colonel F. W. Wormald, D.S.O., and a dismounted party from the 6th Machine Gun Squadron went by bus to Bernes, where they remained in reserve under the 7th Corps.

On the night 7th-8th December, the 3rd Dismounted Division (as it was now called : it actually equalled about three battalions) took over the line from the 17th Infantry Brigade and came under orders of the 24th Division. The sector extended roughly from the Omignon River to Le Verguier (see Map 9 facing page 68). It was a few miles South of the sector held by the Brigade the previous summer. The line consisted of a series of posts with continuous wire. The enemy held a well-wired consecutive trench line running along the ridge to the West of the St. Quentin Canal. The country was bare undulating grass land with a few small woods, and no-man's land varied from 1,000 to 1,500 yards in width. There were many small valleys, sunk roads and much dead ground between our posts and the enemy, and these had constantly to be patrolled. Outstanding features such as Ascension Wood, Big and Little Bill, Victoria X Roads, Fisher Crater, were explored every night. On the night 11th-12th December three prisoners and a machine gun were captured by a patrol of the 3rd Dragoon Guards. The following is a typical example of the work. A patrol of 2 officers and 40 other ranks went out from No. 9 Post at 5 p.m. on 24th December, and reconnoitred Ascension Wood, which was found all clear. The patrol occupied the northern and eastern edges of this wood, scouts being sent forward to Big and Little Bill. At 3.20 a.m. a German patrol was reported approaching Ascension Wood from the North-east. Our patrol waited until the enemy drew close to the wood, when they opened a rapid fire and then charged out on the enemy. Two Germans were taken prisoners.

During most of this period there was snow on the ground, which with bright moonlight made patrolling difficult, though white

suits were provided for use in No Man's Land. The weather 1917
was extremely cold.

On 10th December 87 horses from the Brigade were despatched by rail to Marseilles for transport to Egypt. About this time General Harman rejoined the Brigade, General Vaughan having returned to the Division from England.

On 21st December the Brigade, less the trench party, marched into much the same area occupied before 17th November. Heavy snow followed by a severe frost made this march one of great difficulty.

On 22nd December Major Hon. H. R. Scarlett left the Brigade on promotion to Lieut.-Colonel, and Captain E. T. Boylan rejoining from Headquarters, R.H.A., took over temporary command of " C " Battery.

On 23rd December Captain R. M. Wootten (6th Inniskilling Dragoons) joined the staff of the 3rd Cavalry Division, and Captain D. E. Wallace (2nd Life Guards) became staff captain, being officially appointed to that post three weeks later.

On 31st December General Harman took command of the 3rd Dismounted Division in the trenches, the headquarters of dismounted Brigades and Squadron leaders having also been changed from time to time.

On 1st January Major F. King (commanding 6th Machine Gun 1918 Squadron) left the Brigade to report to Grantham.

On 16th January the 3rd Dismounted Division were relieved by the 1st Dismounted Division, and the 6th Dismounted Brigade (less 5 officers and 200 other ranks) returned to billets by train and lorry. During the relief a train on the Vendelles-Roisel light railway containing mostly 3rd Dragoon Guards ran off the line near Montigny Farm and four trucks overturned resulting in the death of S.S.M. Halliday and L.-Corporal Willis (both 3rd Dragoon Guards), and injury to Lieutenant L. Hellyer (3rd Dragoon Guards) and 14 other ranks.

VADENCOURT AND TERTRY

The party who were not relieved formed part of a pioneer regiment found by the 3rd Cavalry Division. This regiment was billeted at Vendelles and worked in the forward area by night. The Brigade sent up a relieving party the following week.

The battery which on 11th December had moved into an unmade position near Jeancourt remained there until 21st March, covering a zone in front of Sheppard's Copse with S.O.S. barrage at 4,800 yards. Gun positions were concealed and firing was restricted to registration. One gun was put in a forward position near Sheppard's Copse to deal with enemy Tanks. This gun was lost in the first rush on 21st March. Our infantry report that it was still seen firing after they had retired behind it.

On 28th January the Brigade began a three days' march to Tertry. Tertry like all other villages in the devastated area was entirely destroyed and officers and men lived in Nissen and Adrien huts, the horses being in corrugated iron stables. The Royal Dragoons, North Somerset Yeomanry, and 6th Machine Gun Squadron were round Couvigny Farm, Brigade headquarters and the 3rd Dragoon Guards being in Tertry itself with the 6th C.F.A. at Trefcon.

A beginning was at once made on improving huts and stabling, but almost immediately working parties were called for to dig new trench lines. One party worked on the so-called Green Line which ran through Caulaincourt. Another party lived at Jeancourt and worked in the battle zone, a third rode daily to Jeancourt and also worked in the forward area, while a fourth party worked at an aerodrome at Flez. In addition to all this, horses had to be looked after, billets improved, and as much training as possible carried out.

Under the supervision of Lieut.-Colonel F.H.D.C. Whitmore, C.M.G., D.S.O. (Essex Yeomanry), the Cavalry Corps undertook an extensive agricultural scheme. Ploughs and agricultural implements were collected from all parts and repaired by Cavalry Corps Ordnance Work-shops at Estrées. Horses were supplied by the

72

3rd Cavalry Division and work was begun at once in conjunction   1918
with the French, who had a number of tractors.   By the end of
February many acres of land were ploughed and sown with wheat
and other cereals, and some 200 acres were manured and ploughed
ready for potato growing.   The Germans, however, took possession
of these agricultural holdings on Lady Day, 1918.   All the horse
ploughs (but fortunately few of the tractors) were captured.   It
was not until Michaelmas Day, 1918, that the Germans were forced
to relinquish their tenancy.

Night bombing by hostile aircraft was of frequent ·occurrence.
On 18th February the Blues lost 17 horses from a bomb which fell
on one of their stables, and would have lost many more had it not
been for their system of traverses in the stable.

On 4th February Captain C. D. Leyland (1st Life Guards)
arrived and took over command of the 6th Machine Gun Squadron.

On 10th February the Brigade suffered a great loss in the death
of Major G. T. Cliff (second in command, 3rd Dragoon Guards),
who fractured his skull by a fall from his horse, and died at No. 5
C.C.S. at Tincourt.

It was near the end of the month that the break-up of the
Indian Cavalry regiments took place and the 7th Dragoon Guards,
the 6th (Inniskilling) Dragoons and the 17th Lancers came into the
3rd Cavalry Division to replace the Household Cavalry, who were
now under orders to be converted into Machine Gun battalions.*

On 28th February the German offensive which had long been
expected appeared to be imminent.   A German prisoner captured
two days before stated under special examination that there were very
large bodies of troops in the Laon area and for a great distance back.
He described the country as swarming with troops, who were being
slowly moved forward towards the front.   In his own words " it

---

* The Blues had rejoined the 1st and 2nd Life Guards in the 7th Cavalry Brigade
in November, 1917, changing places with the Leicestershire Yeomanry who were
transferred to the 8th Cavalry Brigade.

1918 was like another mobilisation." He considered the attack certain for the 2nd or 3rd March with Paris and Calais as the chief objectives, but he did not know exactly on what front the offensive would be launched.

It is obvious that it was impossible for the Allied Higher Command to be absolutely certain where the main blow would fall, and preparations had therefore to be made to meet the enemy on any part of the front.

On 1st March, according to a pre-arranged plan, part of the 8th Cavalry Brigade moved up into the Brigade area to make room for infantry. Reconnaissances were carried out with a view to moving up to the line quickly in case of emergency. Working parties ceased work, except the party living at Jeancourt, and on 3rd March the Brigade became duty Brigade of Corps Reserve. Major A. S. Barnwell took over command of " C " Battery on 4th March.

During the next two weeks Fervaque Farm, Le Verguier, Vadencourt, Parkers Post and Maissemy were reconnoitred with a view to the organisation of counter attacks.

On 12th March the North Somerset Yeomanry were transferred to the 8th Cavalry Brigade, and the 10th Royal Hussars were transferred to the 6th Cavalry Brigade. The 8th Cavalry Brigade, now temporarily consisting of the Essex, Leicestershire and North Somerset Yeomanry, moved down the following day to the area round Long preparatory to being dismounted. Their future was uncertain. The first proposal was to make them into Cyclist battalions, but it now appeared probable that they would be formed into Machine Gun battalions. It was with genuine regret that the remainder of the Brigade said good-bye to the North Somerset Yeomanry, and the following is the Special Order by Brigadier-General A. E. W. Harman, D.S.O., commanding 6th Cavalry Brigade, dated 12th March, 1918 :—

" After bidding farewell to the officers, non-commissioned

Brigadier-General A. G. Seymour, D. S. O.
Commanded the 6th Cavalry Brigade
March 1918 – August 1918.

"officers, and men of the 1/1st North Somerset Yeomanry, I wish "to put on record the feelings of regret with which all ranks "remaining with the 6th Cavalry Brigade part with the North "Somerset Yeomanry to-day. 1918

"Since 13th November, 1914, when they joined the 6th Cavalry "Brigade, the North Somerset Yeomanry by their high sense of "duty, keenness, and loyalty, by their efficiency in the fighting round "Ypres in November, 1914, February, 1915, April, 1915, on "13th May, 1915, at Loos in September, 1915, at the Hohenzollern "Redoubt January, 1916, and at Monchy-le-Preux April, 1917, "have equally maintained the highest traditions of the Brigade.

"In saying good-bye and wishing them God-speed to-day, I feel "I am voicing the sentiments of all ranks of the Brigade, who, "though losing their comrades-in-arms, will ever retain the true "spirit of friendship in which they have fought and played together "as members of the 6th Cavalry Brigade."

The 10th Royal Hussars on rejoining the Brigade to which they had belonged during the early part of the war, received a very warm welcome.

On 13th March the Brigade moved to the Devise area, where officers and men were in huts and the horses in corrugated iron stables.

The following day Brigadier-General A. G. Seymour, D.S.O., took over command of the 6th Cavalry Brigade in place of Brigadier-General A. E. W. Harman, D.S.O., who shortly afterwards was appointed to command the 3rd Cavalry Division, Captain A. G. M. F. Howard (Duke of Lancaster's Own) becoming A.D.C. to General Seymour instead of Lieutenant H. D. Argles (3rd County of London Yeomanry), who became Camp Commandant, 3rd Cavalry Division.

On 16th March Major H. A. Tomkinson, D.S.O. (Royals) was appointed acting Lieut.-Colonel of the 10th Royal Hussars, and Captain J. C. Humfrey (6th Inniskilling Dragoons) took over command of the 6th Machine Gun Squadron from Captain C. D.

1918 Leyland (1st Life Guards), who rejoined his regiment on its being formed into a Machine Gun battalion.

About this time Captain D. E. Wallace (Staff Captain) left for England to attend the staff course at Cambridge.

On 18th March the Brigade was ordered to find a large digging party for work on rear zone defences. This was subsequently cancelled owing to the German attack.

News was received the following day that the offensive would almost certainly start on the night 20th-21st March and would be preceded by a ten-hours' bombardment.

Throughout the month of March the weather was unusually fine. Every night there was a sharp frost and in the early morning a heavy mist which cleared off about 9.0 a.m. The day was then cloudless and extraordinarily hot for the time of year. In fact the weather could not have been more favourable for the preparation of a great offensive, nor for the first ten days of the attack when it came.

THE GERMAN OFFENSIVE

AT 4.30 a.m. on 21st March the enemy began a heavy 1918 bombardment of practically the whole front held by the 5th and 3rd Armies, and by 10 a.m. a general attack had been launched on a 54-mile front, between the Sensée river on the extreme North and the Oise on the extreme South. An H.V. gun shelled Devise. No. 35 R.A.F. Squadron on the hill above the Brigade camp was shelled out. This shelling must have been at a range of about 18,000 to 20,000 yards.

At 8.15 a.m. came orders to be ready to move at short notice, and at 3.30 p.m. a telegram was received " Stand-to South." The Brigade moved off at 5 p.m., and marching through Croix-Molignaux, Esmery Hallon and Villeselve reached Beaumont (between Ham and Chauny) at 9 p.m. (see Map 10 facing page 78). The weather was fine and frosty, but there was a thick fog. The Brigade bivouacked in the fields.

It should be clearly understood that in the operations which took place during the ensuing five days the 6th Cavalry Brigade was not fighting as a complete unit, but was divided up into five completely separate formations :—(1) the 6th Dismounted Brigade, consisting of about 550 all ranks with 8 machine guns and personnel under Lieut.-Colonel A. Burt, D.S.O. (3rd Dragoon Guards); (2) Brigade headquarters and 6th Signal Troop with Brigadier-General A. G. Seymour, D.S.O., who took command of the 7th and Canadian Dismounted Brigades (the staff of the 6th Cavalry Brigade thereby temporarily performing the duties of a divisional staff); (3) the transport, led horses and horseholders of the Brigade who first went to Pontoise and then to Carlepont: (4) a mounted party of about 12 officers and 150 other ranks, who having been collected from the horse-holders, left Pontoise on 23rd March, and under

77

1918   Major E. H. Watkin Williams (10th Hussars), joined General Harman's detachment (a further mounted party joining Reynold's Force on 26th March); (5) " C " Battery, R.H.A., who, under orders of the 66th Division, were in position at Jeancourt when the great offensive began and fought almost continuously till 9th April.

Orders were received about midnight to form the 6th Dismounted Brigade, and shortly afterwards this party under Colonel Burt (3rd Dragoon Guards) with Captain E. W. T. Miles as second-in-command rode to Ugny-le-Gay. It was a pitch-black night, and the confusion on the roads was considerable. The party went by bus from Ugny-le-Gay to Viry Noureuil, arriving there at 4 a.m. They came under orders of the 3rd Corps, being attached to the 58th Division, and took up a partly dug trench line between Viry Noureuil and Noureuil. Colonel Burt was under the direct command of the G.O.C. 173rd Infantry Brigade.

At 5.30 a.m. on the 22nd Headquarters (6th Cavalry Brigade) marched to Villequier Aumont and General Seymour assumed command of the 3rd Dismounted Division (less 6th Dismounted Brigade). This consisted of the 7th Dismounted Brigade with 8 machine guns, and the Canadian Dismounted Brigade with 12 machine guns. These two Dismounted Brigades moved into huts in the Western part of the Bois de Frières.

Captain G. Babington (North Somerset Yeomanry) joined the 6th Cavalry Brigade as acting Staff Captain early that morning.

Throughout the 22nd the situation remained somewhat obscure. By mid-day the Germans were up at the Crozat canal. The 3rd Corps, which consisted of the 14th, 18th and 58th Divisions, was reinforced by two dismounted Cavalry Divisions. The 2nd Dismounted Cavalry Division was sent to help the 14th Division. The 6th Dismounted Brigade was already with the 58th Division, and during the afternoon the 7th Dismounted Brigade was put at the disposal of the 18th Division, the Canadians being kept in Corps reserve. During the day General Seymour got into touch with forward infantry Brigades, and also supervised the siting of machine guns in Frières Wood. Reconnaissances were made towards Vouel, and close touch was kept with 18th Division headquarters at Ugny. At 8.15 p.m. the 7th Dismounted Brigade was ordered to take up defensive positions along the Eastern edge of Frières Wood. 1918

The 6th Dismounted Brigade had been busy all that day improving their trenches and putting up wire. The 3rd Dragoon Guards were on the right with the 14th Pioneer Battalion on the Southern flank, the Royals in the centre, and the 10th Hussars on the left with the 3rd London Regiment to the North.

During the morning of 23rd March the Germans advanced in great force, and the whole of the 2nd and 3rd Dismounted Cavalry Divisions were heavily engaged.   The 7th and Canadian Brigades (the latter supporting the 54th Infantry Brigade) were obliged to fall back through Frières Wood fighting stubbornly all the way.

The 6th Dismounted Brigade had a day of continuous fighting. Following on a counter-attack made by the 133rd French Regiment on Tergnier and the Butts, the Germans delivered a fresh attack which overwhelmed the French counter-attack and enabled them to break through in masses near the Butts.   Another force broke through further North and rapidly arrived at the North-east entrance of Noureuil, which was the extreme left flank of the Brigade.   Here the enemy were stopped by details of headquarters, consisting of several officers, orderly-room clerks, signallers, cooks, and the mess waiter. The mess itself was captured. The cavalry line, which sustained several heavy local attacks at various points, maintained its position, and officers of the 6th Dismounted Brigade and of the 3rd and 4th London Regiments rallied the French infantry who were falling back. A defensive flank was thrown out and the village was held till dark.

Early in the afternoon of the 23rd, the Headquarters of the Dismounted Division (General Seymour) under orders of the 18th Division, moved to Ugny. A detachment of the 6th C.F.A. under

THE GERMAN OFFENSIVE

Lieut.-Colonel C. H. Stringer did excellent work in assisting the 56th Field Ambulance (18th Division) to clear all wounded from Villequier Aumont before falling back on Ugny.

The Germans continued to advance in great force throughout the afternoon. At 6 p.m. the situation was very serious. It seemed likely the enemy had got right round Villequier Aumont and were advancing through the woods above Ugny. Major-General R. P. Lee, C.B. (18th Division), ordered General Seymour to collect every available man in Ugny and take up a defensive position on the high ground to the North-east of the village. No one had had any sleep for two nights and the men were exhausted after heavy fighting. However, they responded cheerfully to this new demand. By 8.30 p.m. about 2,000 men consisting of dismounted cavalry, elements of various pioneer battalions, infantry details, machine gun detachments, servants and orderlies were in position outside the village and began to dig in. The 7th Dismounted Brigade here rejoined the Division. The enemy, however, did not advance, though there was a certain amount of sniping. Throughout the offensive the Germans seldom attacked after dark. At 9.30 p.m. the French arrived and General Seymour's force was relieved before midnight. During the evening Lieut.-Colonel R. W. Paterson, D.S.O. (Fort Garry Horse) arrived with a mounted detachment from Harman's Force, but finding the gap had been filled by General Seymour he rejoined General Harman next morning.

At 5 a.m. on the 24th the 3rd Dismounted Division with 600 all ranks of the 2nd Dismounted Division marched to Caillouel, and three hours later moved into bivouac immediately West of Dampcourt.

It is difficult to convey any idea of the confusion and uncertainty which prevailed at this stage of the retreat. The Germans were advancing so quickly that at any time they might have appeared on the high ground which hid Chauny from view. They were reported to be already in the woods which covered the steep

range of hills to the North and North-west.   On all sides villages
were in flames and ammunition dumps were sending up huge
columns of black smoke.   Batteries both French and English
galloped across the open country into action.   Armoured cars and
heavy guns in a cloud of dust were passing up and down the roads,
which were already blocked by a ceaseless stream of lorries, tractors,
motor ambulances, British and French troops and civilian refugees.
Walking wounded and small groups of stragglers were making their
way back across the open fields, where, as the German guns moved
up into action, shells began to fall with greater frequency.

During the afternoon Brigadier-General J. E. B. Seely, C.B.,
C.M.G., D.S.O., assumed command of both dismounted Divisions
with headquarters at Appilly, and at the same time the whole force
came under orders of General Diebold commanding the 125th French
Infantry Division, and also the entire sector.   A liaison officer was
sent to live at his headquarters at Varesnes.   Posts were put out
between the Oise canal and the Noyon-Chauny road.

Meanwhile the 6th Dismounted Brigade had been continuously
in action.   At 1 a.m. on the morning of the 24th they received
orders from the 58th Division to withdraw to a line about Chauny.
This was done without incident, although the Germans were only
100 yards distant and three-quarters round the village of Noureuil.
At 3.30 a.m. a line was taken up in the sunk road running North
from Chauny with details of the 3rd London Regiment and the
Oxford Hussars on the right and the 133rd French Infantry Division
on the left.   At 8.30 a.m. the Germans attacked, and under cover
of the mist advanced to within 20 yards, speaking English.   They
were driven back by Hotchkiss and rifle fire.   About 9.30 a.m.
the mist lifted and it was found that the French had moved back.
The order was then received to move to Abbécourt.   This had to be
done over open country under very heavy machine gun fire, the
Germans having advanced round Chauny and forced the French
back on the left.   Practically all the men who had been wounded

were carried in blankets across this open plain for about a mile, being under heavy machine gun and shell fire the whole time. The night was spent lining the canal in the neighbourhood of Manicamp.

At 9.30 a.m. on 25th March, the 6th Dismounted Brigade was ordered by Colonel Pichat to move to the high ground South of Quierzy. This position was occupied, but the Brigade came under heavy shell fire. The Germans must have got direct observation on the column as it left Quierzy, as they followed it up with shelling the whole way, causing many casualties. At 12 noon came orders from the G.O.C. 173rd Infantry Brigade to re-occupy Quierzy. But instructions had been received that orders were to come from the French only. This dual control proved unworkable. Quierzy, however, was occupied by half the dismounted Brigade, the remainder being held in reserve.

Early the same morning (25th) the 2nd Dismounted Division were withdrawn to their horses and the 3rd Dismounted Division under orders from General Diebold took up a defensive position from Mondescourt to the canal, a detachment of Canadians being sent to help Colonel Pichat at Petit Quierzy.

At 11 a.m., under orders of the 3rd Corps, all the dismounted cavalry (except the 6th Brigade) were withdrawn from the line and marched back to the horses at Carlepont. The enemy occupied Appilly about 1.30 p.m., crossed the canal and took up a position North of the Oise.

The night was spent at Carlepont and the following day the 3rd Cavalry Division (less the 6th Dismounted Brigade and Harman's detachment) marched to Choisy-au-Bac at the junction of the Oise and the Aisne about 2 miles from Compiègne.

It was found impossible to extricate the 6th Dismounted Brigade till the morning of the 26th, when they marched to Besme, and then to Tracy-le-Mons, being inspected on the way by the G.O.C. 58th Division (Major-General A. B. E. Cator, D.S.O.), who

THE GERMAN OFFENSIVE

expressed his satisfaction at the work carried out by the Brigade 1918 during these four days of continuous fighting. The following is General Cator's Order, which was read to all ranks concerned :—
" My warmest thanks and congratulations to you and all ranks
" of the 3rd Cavalry Division on the splendid work you have done
" in the XIXth Corps. The fighting spirit and determination dis-
" played have been beyond all praise, and the results achieved have
" been of the greatest value."

On 27th March the 6th Dismounted Brigade rejoined at Choisy-au-Bac, having covered a very long distance on foot since the battle started—from La Fère almost to Compiègne. On the same day General Harman's mounted detachment, of whose doings during the opening days of the German offensive it is now necessary to give some account, rejoined the Brigade (see Map 10 facing page 78).

At 9.50 a.m. on 23rd March, General Harman, who commanded what was left of the 3rd Cavalry Division (not to be confused with the 3rd Dismounted Division) was notified by telephone that the Germans had broken through the line at Ham and was ordered to turn out as many mounted men as possible. To this force the 6th Cavalry Brigade contributed 12 officers and 150 men under Major E. H. Watkin Williams (10th Hussars). The men were raised from the horseholders, who at the ratio of one man to four horses were all that remained of the 3rd Cavalry Division after the dismounted party under Colonel Burt had left. On reporting at 3rd Corps headquarters at Buchoire, General Harman was ordered to take command of the mounted detachments of the 2nd and 3rd Cavalry Divisions (about 750 mounted men in all), also of Colonel Theobald's infantry (600 strong), a detachment of No. 13 Balloon Company (8 Lewis guns and personnel), "O" Battery R.H.A., one lorry and one tender. The whole force was to be known as " Harman's detachment." By 1 p.m. it was concentrated in readiness at Berlancourt, being joined during the afternoon by Colonel

THE GERMAN OFFENSIVE

Theobald's force. Patrols were sent out to Esmery Hallon, Ham, Muille Villette, Brouchy and Ollezy to get in touch with the enemy. The same evening mounted detachments were sent to fill the gap between Villequier Aumont and La Neuville, but finding General Seymour's force already there (as recounted above) they returned to Berlancourt early on the 24th March, and during the morning, in order to protect the left flank of the 14th Division, took up a position North-east of Villeselve in touch with Theobald's infantry, who were blocking the Western exits of the village. The 2nd Cavalry Division mounted detachment was sent to clear up the position between Esmery Hallon and Golancourt.

About 2 p.m. on the 24th, the 6th Cavalry Brigade mounted detachment, which was then at Berlancourt, was ordered by Lieut.-Colonel R. W. Paterson, D.S.O. (Fort Garry Horse), who commanded the 3rd Cavalry Division detachment, to make a mounted attack on some hostile infantry and machine guns on the line Hill 81 —Copse A—Copse B (see Map 11 facing page 84). The infantry were very shaky, and it was hoped that a successful mounted attack would regain some of the ground which had been lost, and also restore confidence.

The detachment (roughly equal in numbers to a squadron) moved along the main road to Villeselve, taking the sunken track running North into Collezy. On approaching Collezy the Squadron came under heavy machine gun fire from the direction of Golancourt, but got under cover of a large farm at the South-east exit of the village.

The Squadron which was under the command of Major E. H. Watkin Williams (10th Hussars) with Captain C. W. Turner (Royals) second in command was formed into three troops by regiments, the 3rd Dragoon Guards under Lieutenant A. B. P. L. Vincent, M.C., the 10th Royal Hussars under Lieutenant Viscount Ednam, and The Royal Dragoons under Lieutenant the Hon. W. H. Cubitt.

THE GERMAN OFFENSIVE

The plan of attack had been explained to troop leaders on the way. Lieutenant Vincent was ordered to move towards Copse " B." He was to charge any Germans he encountered and secure the right flank. The 10th Hussars and Royals were to make the main attack towards Copse " A."

The 3rd Dragoon Guards moved off immediately, and almost at once came under machine gun fire. They advanced at a steady pace and soon encountered parties of German infantry, some of whom ran into the Copse where they were followed on foot. Many were shot at point blank range as they ran away. Twelve prisoners were handed over to the infantry and the right flank was secured.

As soon as the 3rd Dragoon Guards were on their way the 10th Hussars and Royals started. The formation was troops in line, first the 10th Hussars, then the Royals about 150 yards behind. When the charge started the men were knee to knee, but owing to machine gun fire and the fast pace they tended to open out and by the time the enemy was reached were more or less extended.

On clearing the farm the head of the column wheeled slightly to the left and passed through a few scattered parties of our infantry. The Germans were then clearly seen in front of Copse "A." The distance to be covered was about 600 yards, the last 200 yards being over plough. There was considerable machine gun fire from the left flank.

The 10th Hussars advanced steadily and when the enemy saw mounted troops making straight for them and heard the men cheering, they began to surrender freely. The 10th Hussars rode straight through the enemy, the Royals following and mopping up small parties who had run together. After the mêlée, " Rally " was sounded, prisoners were collected, and the Squadron returned to the main Berlancourt—Villeselve road, wounded being picked up. Ninety-five prisoners were brought in by the 10th Hussars and the Royals, making a total of 107 in all. The number, however, was really greater, as small bodies of the enemy kept giving them-

85

selves up to the infantry who followed up the charge.   One machine gun was brought back intact, one was presented to the Commander of the French infantry, and one was put out of action.   The machine gun on the left flank was not captured as owing to the heavy plough it was able to get away just in time.   Besides the prisoners, between 70 and 100 Germans were sabred.   The casualties of the Squadron were about 73 out of 150, but comparatively few were killed. Lieutenant Hon. W. H. Cubitt (Royals) was mortally wounded during the attack, whereby one of the most promising young officers in the Brigade was lost.

The whole operation though small in itself is a brilliant proof of what cavalry can do when they have the chance of being used in their proper capacity.   Probably no better example of the value of shock action could be found in the history of the whole war. The manœuvre gave the infantry renewed confidence, and they were able to push forward their line well beyond the limits of the charge, thus enabling the remnants of two battalions who had been fighting near Cugny to retire on Villeselve and re-form.   Demoralisation of the enemy, encouragement of our own tired troops, the immediate capture of important ground—these are solid advantages which the expert soldier has always realised cavalry could give.   But the opportunities have been few.   All the more pity that on 21st March two-thirds of the three cavalry divisions available had to be thrown into the battle on foot.

At 4.55 p.m. on the 24th, Harman's detachment was ordered to withdraw to Guiscard, mounted troops covering the retirement of all infantry in the district.

The enemy were now developing a determined attack in a Southerly direction on a rough line—Montdidier—Lassigny—Noyon—Appilly.   It was of the utmost importance to prevent him breaking through between Lassigny and Noyon, so that the salient formed by the Oise immediately South of Noyon might hold out (see Map 10 facing page 78).   In this work the cavalry played a most effective part.

THE GERMAN OFFENSIVE

Throughout the night of 24th - 25th March Harman's detachment was active, and at 1.30 p.m. on the 25th it came under orders of the 10th French Division. During the afternoon the 2nd and 3rd Cavalry Division detachments went up to Munrancourt to support the French. About 6 p.m. the French began to fall back, and the cavalry were ordered to cover their retirement.

Early on 26th March a further force was collected from all available mounted men at Carlepont, the 6th Cavalry Brigade finding 5 officers and 89 other ranks. They joined what was called Reynolds' Force,* coming under the orders of Lieut.-Colonel A. B. Reynolds (12th Lancers, commanding the Northumberland Hussars). From the 27th to the 29th this force was employed patrolling the line Chiry—Thiescourt—Lassigny—Canny—Biermont. This front was now held entirely by French troops, supported by British artillery. The information obtained by the cavalry patrols as to the position of the French and enemy forces was of great value to the artillery (see Map 10 facing page 78).

Meanwhile, at 3.30 a.m. on 26th March Harman's detachment withdrew through the French infantry to reserve at Dives. But at 9.50 a.m. the enemy being reported in the Bois des Essarts, the 2nd Cavalry Division detachment were ordered to take up a position at Charbonneaux Farm and at 10.35 a.m. orders were given to the 3rd Cavalry Division detachment to push the enemy out of the Bois des Essarts and Mont de Porquericourt. This was done successfully, the attack being made by the Canadian and part of the 7th Cavalry Brigade detachments. The remainder of the 7th Cavalry Brigade and the 6th Cavalry Brigade detachment protected the right flank by holding the Bois de la Reserve. Touch was obtained with the 2nd Cavalry Division and a continuous line to Lagny established. The Germans, however, crossed the river at Catigny and broke

---

* During the night 24th-25th March, Colonel Reynolds drew 120 horses from the led horses of the 3rd Cavalry Division, and with the 120 men of his regiment thus mounted joined Harman's detachment at 8 a.m. on the 25th.

1918   through the French line near Candor, thus turning the left flank of the 2nd Cavalry Division, who were compelled to withdraw to Dives. This in turn exposed the left flank of the 3rd Cavalry Division detachment. The 6th Cavalry Brigade detachment was therefore ordered to push forward mounted to support the 2nd Cavalry Division (16th Lancers) and were the last troops to withdraw. Led horses were sent back and the 2nd Cavalry Division informed that the 3rd Cavalry Division would protect their left flank. A rearguard action was then fought on foot, a determined stand being made at Cuy, which enabled the 6th Cavalry Brigade to get clear. The action was continued over the Bois de la Reserve, the 3rd Cavalry Division detachment finally crossing the river at Evricourt, where the French had dug themselves in.

Harman's detachment then received orders to withdraw to Thiescourt and from there went into reserve at Elincourt late on the evening of the 26th.

On 27th March the whole force broke up and the 3rd Cavalry Division detachment (less those who formed part of Reynolds' Force) joined the dismounted parties at Choisy-au-Bac.

Throughout this period, whether working with mounted or dismounted detachments, the 6th C.F.A. never failed to evacuate all wounded. In spite of the fact that casualty clearing stations were constantly moving back, and it became almost impossible to obtain accurate information with regard to the location of medical units, the 6th C.F.A. passed back large numbers of wounded first to Noyon and later to a French Hospital at Compiègne.

The Brigade, either mounted or dismounted, had been marching and fighting continuously since 21st March. It now remained at Choisy-au-Bac for three days. The horses were on the edge of the forest of Compiègne, about a mile South of Choisy-au-Bac, and the men in bivouac alongside. On the night 27th-28th there was a severe bombing attack by hostile aircraft, one man being killed and a number of men and horses wounded.

THE GERMAN OFFENSIVE

On 29th March the detachment from Reynolds' Force rejoined and, except for the absence of " C " Battery, the 6th Cavalry Brigade was once more a complete mounted fighting force.   The following statement appeared in the Commander-in-Chief's despatch of 30th March : —

" During the past week our cavalry have fought with great " gallantry, both mounted and dismounted, and have repulsed the " enemy, inflicting heavy losses on him in numerous engagements."

The whole line from Montdidier to the Oise canal at Sempigny now seemed more secure and the danger point shifted to Amiens.

CHAPTER XI

VILLERS BRETONNEUX

1918

O N 29th March the Brigade marched through Compiègne and Arsy to Clermont, and then to Airion for the night. The area was crowded. In the small farm allotted to Brigade headquarters there were also a squadron of French Dragoons and a working party of 300 Italians. Late that night General Seymour attended a conference at Divisional headquarters near St. Just-en-Chaussée.

On 30th March the Brigade made a long trek of 35 miles through St. Just-en-Chaussée and Berny to Sains-les-Amiennois. All three regiments the Machine Gun Squadron and 6th C.F.A., in addition to the 7th Cavalry Brigade, were in bivouac in and around a gigantic farm on the outskirts of the woods one-and-a-half miles South-east of Sains. It poured with rain throughout the march and during the night.

That evening Lieutenant R. Heyworth Savage (Royals) joined Brigade headquarters as Brigade Signalling Officer, in place of Captain R. S. Stancliffe (2nd Life Guards), who had been promoted to command the 3rd Signal Squadron.

The Brigade remained at Sains over Easter Sunday, and on Monday, 1st April, moved at 6 a.m. through Boves to the Bois de Gentelles in support of the 2nd Cavalry Division who (with the Canadian Cavalry Brigade attached and later with the 7th Cavalry Brigade) were engaged in Rifle Wood, South-east of Hourges. Patrols were sent out to Morgemont Wood and also towards Marcelcave and a liaison officer was sent to the 2nd Cavalry Division. The Brigade remained in readiness all day and passed the night in Tronville Wood (1,000 yards West of the Bois de Blangy). The 2nd April was spent in bivouac, further patrols being sent out to get in touch with the infantry. At 8 p.m. that night the Royals marched to a concealed position about 1,500 yards North-west of Villers Bretonneux, and then went forward to dig a series of strong points in the neighbourhood of the Bois de Vaire. Early on 3rd April the 3rd Dragoon Guards and Machine Gun Squadron marched to the Bois l'Abbé, the Royals also returning there after digging. Brigade headquarters and the 10th Hussars marched to Fouilloy, the whole Brigade coming under orders of the 1st Cavalry Division. The 6th C.F.A. was at Blangy-Tronville. On 3rd April the 14th Infantry Division relieved the 1st Cavalry Division, and the Brigade was ordered to remain in reserve to the 14th Division. The Royals worked again at the same line of strong points during the night.

At 5.30 a.m. on 4th April, the enemy opened a heavy bombardment on the whole front of the 14th Division, who had only taken over the line a few hours before after heavy fighting further South. Fouilloy was shelled, and at 6.30 a.m. the G.O.C. 14th Division moved his headquarters to the Orphanage on the Fouilloy—Blangy-Tronville road, General Seymour and his staff moving there simultaneously. The enemy attacked about 6.15 a.m. and our infantry were forced back from the front line posts. It was essential for the defence of Villers Bretonneux (and of Amiens) that the high ground on both sides of the Fouilloy—Warfusée road should be held. The 43rd Infantry Brigade was ordered to move up into position on this high ground, and shortly afterwards (about 7.15 a.m.) the 10th Hussars with 4 machine guns were ordered to operate on their left flank (North of the Fouilloy—Warfusée road) and the 3rd Dragoon Guards and the Royals with 8 machine guns on their right flank (North-east of Villers Bretonneux). In the event of the infantry not having arrived on this high ground, it was to be held by the cavalry at all costs. Meanwhile the bivouac of the Royals and Machine Gun Squadron in the Bois l'Abbé had been heavily shelled, and they had been forced to move out into the valley between the wood and Fouilloy.

The 10th Hussars moved up without delay on the left flank, and shortly afterwards the 3rd Dragoon Guards followed by the Royals came up on the right.   All three regiments advanced mounted at a fast pace, and the Royals and 10th Hussars came into action immediately, one squadron of the 3rd Dragoon Guards forming a defensive flank.   All horses were sent back, and the men fought dismounted.   The Germans were attempting to advance all along the line, and there was a gap, both on the left flank between what remained of the 41st and 42nd Infantry Brigades and on the right flank between the 41st Infantry Brigade and the Australians.   Both these gaps were filled, that on the left by the 10th Hussars and that on the right by the Royals. The situation on the right was only just saved in time.   The Germans were attempting to push forward in large numbers and " B " Squadron (Royals) (Captain C. W. Turner, M.C.) at once took up a position just North of the main Amiens— St. Quentin road, being shortly afterwards reinforced by "A" Squadron (Captain E. W. T. Miles, M.C.).   There was still a considerable gap which was temporarily held by the R.S.M. and headquarter orderlies of the regiment until " C " Squadron (Captain W. P. Browne, M.C.) came up to relieve them.   At 11.45 Brigade headquarters moved to a point about 500 yards North of Villers Bretonneux, and divisional headquarters moved up to the Orphanage at Fouilloy.   By mid-day the situation was in hand and the cavalry with elements of the 14th Division held a more or less definite line from Vaire-sous-Corbie, West of the Bois de Vaire to a point about 1,000 yards East of Villers Bretonneux on the main Amiens—St. Quentin road.

The work done by the 6th Cavalry Brigade on the morning of 4th April is undoubtedly one of the finest examples of the value of a mounted mobile reserve which the whole war has to offer. Villers Bretonneux was the key to Amiens and the Germans fully realised that fact, as was proved by the several attempts which they

VILLERS BRETONNEUX

made on later occasions to take and hold the place. When the 6th Cavalry Brigade came into action about 8.0 a.m. that morning the way to Villers Bretonneux lay open, and the Germans were advancing quickly. It was not a question even of an hour or two. It was a question of minutes. The only roads by which infantry in lorries could have been rushed up were under concentrated shell fire. None but mounted troops moving quickly over open country could have saved the situation.

During the morning the 7th Cavalry Brigade had moved up into a position of readiness and a squadron of the 17th Lancers was sent to reinforce " B " Squadron of the Royals, who were in touch with the Australians on their right. The enemy were several times reported to be massing for attack, and the 14th Divisional artillery dealt with these targets. At 1.45 p.m. the 10th Hussars reported that a heavy attack was developing between the Bois de Vaire and Hamel. Machine gun and rifle fire largely stopped this attack which broke down completely.

The 6th C.F.A. were in the Chateau just West of the Bois l'Abbé. A medical officer and bearers were in direct touch with headquarters of regiments, and both cavalry and Australian wounded were evacuated down the main road in motor ambulances which were able to pass right up through Villers Bretonneux.

At 2.15 p.m. the 7th Dragoon Guards with 4 machine guns were sent to reinforce the 10th Hussars. At 5.30 p.m. the Australians began to move back on the right flank. This was reported by Colonel Wormald, who attempted to ascertain the reason for their withdrawal. The squadron of the 17th Lancers, which was already in support to the Royals, moved forward at the gallop and formed a defensive flank and as soon as the two remaining squadrons of the 17th Lancers came up they occupied the posts immediately North of the Villers Bretonneux—Warfusée road. Meanwhile Captain S. G. Howes, M.C. (Brigade Major) was sent to gain touch with the Australian headquarters, and the Australians, who had withdrawn entirely through a misunderstanding, at once resumed their former positions. By 7 p.m. the situation was quiet. Heavy rain fell throughout the day and continued during the night. There was no cover of any kind. Conditions could hardly have been worse.

During the night the 3rd Cavalry Division with the 15th Australian Brigade relieved the 14th Division, of which two Brigades had suffered very heavy casualties. The 6th Cavalry Brigade with the Inniskilling Dragoons and the 17th Lancers, held the right sector from the Fouilloy—Warfusée road to the Villers Bretonneux—Warfusée road, the 7th Dragoon Guards being in reserve. All horses were sent back to Tronville Wood. At 8 a.m. on 5th April, the valley where Brigade headquarters was situated was shelled, and headquarters moved to a quarry about 1,000 yards South of Fouilloy. At 10.45 a.m. the enemy opened a heavy bombardment on the whole sector which continued for three-quarters of an hour, and was accompanied by an accurate indirect machine gun barrage. The enemy, who attempted to attack under cover of this bombardment, were held up by our artillery and machine gun fire, but appeared in considerable force on the sky line about 900 yards from our posts and began to dig in. This excellent target was satisfactorily dealt with by our artillery.

At 2 p.m. a message was received from the 3rd Cavalry Division, saying that the Australian battalion on the left reported the enemy appeared to be massing along the whole front. This attack however, never developed. The rest of the day passed quietly, and at 10.30 p.m. the relief of the 6th and 7th Cavalry Brigades by the Australians began, being completed by 3.30 a.m.

All regiments were back in Tronville Wood by 5 a.m. on 6th April, and at 9.30 a.m. the Brigade (less the Machine Gun Squadron, who remained another 24 hours in the line) marched into billets at Camon.

VILLERS BRETONNEUX

The casualties during the last two weeks were :—
Brigade Headquarters (including 6th Signal Troop and 13th
M.V.S.) : Other ranks, 2 killed, 6 wounded. 3rd Dragoon
Guards : Officers, Lieutenant N. T. King (killed), Lieutenant F. B.
Katinakis (died of wounds), Lieutenant T. Kohler, Captain R. B.
Allen, Lieutenant R. D. Younger, Lieutenant M. J. Clery
(wounded); other ranks, 25 killed, 51 wounded, 13 missing. The
Royal Dragoons : Officers, Lieutenant Hon. W. H. Cubitt (died of
wounds), Captain H. McCall Johnson (A.V.C.) (died of wounds),
Lieutenant A. R. Cooper, Lieutenant D'A. F. Harris, Lieutenant
E. St. G. Stedall (wounded); other ranks, 17 killed, 59 wounded,
8 missing. 10th Hussars : Officers, 2nd-Lieutenant R. G. Field
(killed), Lieut.-Colonel H. A. Tomkinson, D.S.O., Major
E. H. Watkin Williams, Captain E. W. E. Palmes, M.C.,
Lieutenant Viscount Ednam, M.C., Lieutenant W. J. Brisley,
Lieutenant F. R. Gaskell, 2nd-Lieutenant H. D. Kelleway
(wounded); other ranks, 9 killed, 61 wounded, 15 missing. 6th
Machine Gun Squadron : Officers, Captain F. B. Ratcliffe (died of
wounds), Lieutenant G. H. Eaton (killed), Lieutenant J. A. Wilkes
(missing, believed killed), Lieutenant A. Cole, Lieutenant A. W. G.
Windham, 2nd-Lieutenant R. C. Hollis (wounded); other ranks,
2 killed, 29 wounded, 4 missing. 6th C.F.A. : Officers, Captain
A. W. Forrest (wounded); other ranks, 1 killed, 12 wounded.

On 6th April reinforcements from the North Somerset
Yeomanry, whose conversion into a dismounted force had not been
proceeded with owing to the offensive, arrived, and officers and
men were allotted to the three regiments. The Brigade was
extremely fortunate in receiving this excellent personnel at a time
when it was so much needed. Of the officers who returned, Captain
A. B . Mitchell and Captain A. W. Phipps had been with the
North Somerset Yeomanry throughout the war. Lieut.-Colonel
F. H. D. C. Whitmore, C.M.G., D.S.O., took over command of
the 10th Royal Hussars.

VILLERS BRETONNEUX

The Brigade remained at Camon from 6th April to 11th April, and was fully occupied in reorganising and refitting.

It is perhaps worth recording that on the first day of the battle (March 21st) at least 64 German divisions took part in the operations. This number considerably exceeded the total forces composing the entire British Army in France.   The British forces on the original battle front on the morning of 21st March consisted of 25 infantry divisions and three cavalry divisions.

Some short account must now be given of the doings of " C " Battery from 21st March to this date (see Map 9 facing page 68).

When the barrage started on 21st March, " C " Battery, who were in position near Jeancourt, immediately opened fire on S.O.S. lines.   Owing to the fog, together with the smoke and gas, great difficulty was experienced in laying.   Within half-an-hour the only communication with the rear was by runners.   The group telephone exchange was destroyed by a direct hit.   Visual signalling was impossible owing to the fog.   About 1.30 p.m. the fog lifted and Germans crossing the ridge by Grand Priel Wood were engaged over open sights.   Several of the gun pits were blown in, but the guns moved into the open and remained in action, until about 5.45 p.m., when the battery was ordered to withdraw a section at a time.   An anti-tank gun with all available shrapnel was left behind until dusk. The battery withdrew to a position on the Vendelles—Bernes road, and on 22nd March marched to St. Christ, then back to Bouvincourt (occupying various positions on the way) where it came into action.   During the night the Battery was withdrawn again and during the morning of the 23rd it fought several rear-guard actions notably on the slope West of Brie, where with the 16th Brigade it had excellent shooting over open sights.   As it retired from this open position and crossed the Somme near Brie, the battery came under heavy fire from three or four enemy batteries and a large flight of aeroplanes.   A covered position was finally

VILLERS BRETONNEUX

taken up West of Briost to cover the crossing at St. Christ. The battery was in action throughout the night and on 24th March moved to a position West of Barleux. Here Captain E. T. Boylan, M.C., took over temporary command, Major Barnwell going to command the 4th Brigade R.H.A. in the absence of Colonel A. R. Wainewright. At 1 p.m. the enemy were advancing in force on Barleux, and the battery received orders to withdraw to Assevillers, from where it had excellent targets, moving at dusk to Dompierre.

On 25th March the battery, which was in support of a Brigade of the 66th Division acting as rearguard to the main body, did considerable execution on the enemy advancing between Assevillers and Dompierre, and about 10 a.m. retired to a second position South of Chuignes to prevent the enemy molesting the rearguard marching down the main road from Villers Carbonnel to Villers Bretonneux. As soon as the rearguard had passed Foucaucourt the battery was ordered to go into action just North of Harbonnières (see Map 13 facing page 104).

On the morning of the 26th the enemy continued his attack and the battery fired continuously at hostile waves of infantry crossing the high ground East of Vauvillers, occupying a new position West of Harbonnières about mid-day and remaining in action till dusk. Major Barnwell again took command of the battery.

Before dawn on the 27th the battery was ordered to rendezvous South of Guillaucourt, showing no lights and making as little noise as possible, as the enemy were reported in Bayonvillers on the right rear. The Luce was then crossed at Ignaucourt and a position taken up with " G " and " K " Batteries South of Cayeux, covering the high ground on the North of the river. Here the enemy were engaged and driven back. That evening a further withdrawal was ordered, first to Ignaucourt then to Hangard.

On 28th March the battery fired from this position, and about mid-day received orders to retire to Villers Bretonneux, where it

1918   came into action in the station yard. " G " and " K " Batteries being withdrawn, " C " Battery was now the foremost battery of artillery on this sector. On 2nd April Captain Boylan again took over command.

On the morning of 4th April the enemy attacked, the preliminary bombardment being very heavy on the station. Observation was impossible owing to the thick mist, and all firing had to be done from the map until the afternoon, when the visibility improved. The guns and wagon lines suffered severely, one complete detachment being killed by a 5.9. About 4 p.m. our infantry began to come over the ridge 400 yards in front of the battery, which was ordered to retire. There were then only one officer and 15 men to man 5 guns. Many of the horses had been hit, and it was with difficulty that teams could be put together to pull the guns out through the mud, before the enemy appeared on the ridge in front. An open position was then taken up South of Cachy covering Hangard Wood.

On 5th April the battery moved to the P.O.W. cage just East of the Bois l'Abbé, and during the night a sudden burst of fire killed three men, wounded eighteen, and hit a large number of horses, throwing the teams into confusion. A stampede from a Field Battery's wagon lines almost started " C " Battery's horses, but owing to the excellent work of the drivers the stampede was prevented.

On 9th April the battery marched to the rear wagon lines at Cagny, having lost since 21st March almost 50 per cent. of its strength in men and horses. No guns were lost except the one in the forward position on the first day of the offensive.

During these operations the following officers of the Battery were wounded : Lieutenant R. Patrick, Lieutenant R. L. Hutchins, Lieutenant T. Stevens, 2nd-Lieutenant O. L. Boord, 2nd-Lieutenant M. H. Cooper.

VILLERS BRETONNEUX

On the morning of 9th April began the German offensive from the La Bassée canal to Bois Grenier developing further North against Messines the following morning. Throughout 10th April the 6th Cavalry Brigade stood-to at short notice, and early on 11th April marched through Amiens and Auxi-le-Chateau to the Buire-au-Bois area, continuing the march the following day and arriving late at night in billets at Conteville—Hestrus—Eps. While the Brigade was watering at Wavrans in the dark, hostile aircraft appeared overhead and tried to hit the St. Pol-Hesdin railway. Several bombs fell about 50 yards from the horses without doing any damage.

At 6 a.m. on 13th April, the Brigade concentrated at Bailleul-les-Pernes, and later in the day billeted there and at Ferfay and Aumerval. Merville had been taken on 11th April, and the line now ran immediately East of the Forest of Nieppe and then Southwards about 2 miles East of St. Venant.

The Brigade remained in this area during the next ten days, standing-to every morning at 6 a.m. ready to move up in support of the XIth Corps. The reserve and support lines from Haverskerque to Les Amusoires with roads and lines of approach were thoroughly reconnoitred by General Seymour and all senior officers. "C" Battery rejoined from Cagny.

On 16th April Lieut.-Colonel A. Burt, D.S.O., left the Brigade to become G.O.C. 7th Cavalry Brigade, and Lieut.-Colonel C. L. Rome, D.S.O. (11th Hussars), assumed command of the 3rd Dragoon Guards. About this time Major A. S. Barnwell, D.S.O. ("C" Battery), was seriously injured by a fall from his horse and was evacuated. On 24th April Brigade headquarters with the 6th C.F.A. and the 13th M.V.S. moved to Fontaine-les-Hermans, and the Royals to Nedonchelle.

On 4th May the Brigade began a three days' trek Southwards, and marching through St. Pol and Doullens arrived on the afternoon of 6th May at Contay. Here all units were in bivouac, and came

1918   into 4th Army Reserve in 3rd Corps area. The enemy were expected to attack very shortly on this sector. The Brigade stood-to every morning at 5 a.m. Conferences were held with infantry commanders, plans worked out for holding important tactical features (such as Henencourt and Laviéville) and the whole sector was frequently reconnoitred by General Seymour, and all unit commanders. Every other night the Brigade found strong digging parties for work on the line East of Henencourt.

On 12th May Captain S. G. Howes, M.C., after having been on the Brigade Staff for over three years, first as Staff Captain, then as Brigade Major, was appointed G.S.O.2 of the 3rd Cavalry Division, and Captain E. A. Fielden, M.C. (10th Hussars), became Brigade Major in his place.

On 17th May the Brigade marched to Belloy-sur-Somme. The three regiments and machine gun squadron were in bivouac in the Bois de Belloy, the ambulance and battery being in the village.

On Sunday, 19th May, after a short Church parade, the Corps Commander (Lieut.-General Sir C. T. McM. Kavanagh, K.C.B., C.V.O., D.S.O.) presented medals awarded to officers and men since 21st March. An Australian band played during the ceremony.

On 20th May Major D. Scott, M.C., took over command of " C " Battery.

During the next ten days the Brigade carried out mounted and dismounted training. The weather which had been unusually fine for several weeks remained extremely hot.

On 27th May the Germans attacked between Chavignon and Berry-au-Bac and within 4 days reached the Marne.

On 31st May the Brigade marched to Behencourt and went into bivouac in the wood West of the village and along the banks of the River Hallue. Throughout this period the Germans were expected to attack. At 4 p.m. on 6th June a G.H.Q. telegram was received saying a German offensive between Montdidier and the

Oise was probable within the next two days and a simultaneous **1918**
attack on this front possible.

Orders having been received that the Brigade might be called
upon to support the 31st French Corps in the Moreuil sector, bridges
and roads in this direction were carefully reconnoitred. The attack
between Montdidier and the Oise took place on the 9th, but the
4th Army front remained quiet.

On 14th June the Brigade moved back to Belloy, and the
following day General Seymour with other officers reconnoitred the
ground round the Bois de Gentelles in the event of the French
needing support.

The Brigade remained at Belloy, but little work could be done
owing to an epidemic of so-called P.U.O. This disease appeared
to be a virulent type of influenza, and was accompanied by high
temperature and often by serious after-effects. Lieut.-Colonel
C. H. Stringer, D.S.O. (O.C. 6th C.F.A.), formed a special hospital
under canvas at Belloy, where by the end of the month there were
close upon 500 cases undergoing treatment.

On 25th June the Brigade moved to the Le Mesge—Soues—
Riencourt area. On 29th June Captain E. A. Fielden, M.C., left
for England to attend the staff course at Cambridge, and Captain
D. E. Wallace, M.C., on his return from this course a few days
later, became Brigade Major during his absence.

On 4th July "C" Battery (under Lieutenant A. A. Bontor,
M.C.) supported the attack of the Australians on Hamel, and came
into action near Heilly. The Battery fired a barrage at zero for four
hours. It remained in this area until July 11th and fired almost
every night.

The Brigade remained in the same area throughout July and
carried out training. The P.U.O. epidemic had almost subsided
by the middle of the month. On 15th July the Reverend A.
Rowland Grant, M.V.O., joined the Brigade as Chaplain.

CHAPTER XII

THE ALLIED OFFENSIVE

GENERAL SEYMOUR attended a conference at Cavalry Corps headquarters on Sunday 4th August, and the plans for the offensive of 8th August, which had been kept absolutely secret, were explained.

On 6th August at 10.30 p.m. the Brigade marched to Renancourt, and remained there during the following day. At 9.30 p.m. on 7th August, the Brigade marched to the assembly area (1,000 yards West of Tronville Wood). Considerable delay was experienced in Amiens shortly before midnight owing to Tanks on the road.

The battle which began on 8th August not only freed Amiens and the Paris-Amiens railway, but proved to be the first of a series of tremendous battles which only ended three months later (on 11th November), when the enemy, completely broken and in rout, was forced to sign an unconditional armistice.

The operations of 8th August may be summarised thus:— The 4th Army was attacking the German positions between Morlancourt and the Amiens—Roye road, the 1st French Army operating to the South. There were two objectives which affected the Cavalry:

(1) The *Red* Line: Mézières—Cayeux—West of Harbonniéres; (2) The *Blue* Line: East of Le Quesnel—East of Caix— East of Harbonniéres (see Map 13 facing page 104).

The 3rd Cavalry Division was to work with the 1st and 3rd Canadian Infantry Divisions till the Red Line was reached (the 1st Cavalry Division working with the 2nd Canadian and 5th Australian Divisions to the North of the railway) and was then to pass through the infantry and seize and hold the Blue Line, exploiting any success to the East of it, if possible.

THE ALLIED OFFENSIVE

The morning was dry and foggy. The attack of the infantry in conjunction with numerous Tanks proved a complete surprise, and went well from the start.

At 5.40 a.m. the Brigade followed the 7th Cavalry Brigade up the cavalry track which led almost due East, skirting Cachy on the North and crossing the front line about 1,000 yards East of that village. The Brigade halted just outside Cachy until 9.30 a.m. and then advanced to a point East of Morgemont Wood. At 10.50 the Brigade moved down into the Luce valley and crossing the river at Demuin passed shortly afterwards through the infantry.

The Canadian Cavalry Brigade was now fighting in and about Beaucourt, and the 7th Cavalry Brigade took Cayeux Wood at the gallop, rounding up over 200 prisoners and taking several machine guns. The taking of Cayeux Wood in the face of strong opposition was a brilliant piece of work and is yet another example of what can be done by cavalry in open warfare.

At 1 p.m. the Royals with 4 machine guns were sent to support the 7th Cavalry Brigade. "C" Battery came into action near Beaucourt. At 1.45 p.m. the Brigade was ordered to push forward towards Le Quesnel, but this order was cancelled, the Royals remaining with the 7th Cavalry Brigade. A little later the remainder of the 6th Brigade also moved over to the left flank. The Royals had received verbal instructions to push forward in support of the 17th Lancers, who had been ordered to advance towards the Vrély—Warvillers road. On the arrival of the remainder of the 6th Brigade East of Cayeux Wood, General Seymour immediately sent on the 10th Hussars to support the Royals, who had reached the Wood (E15) 1,500 yards South of Caix, but were unable to advance further owing to the fact that the high ground from Beaufort to Le Quesnel on their right and the Blue Line West of Beaufort were strongly held by the enemy. The 10th Hussars were also unable to advance, but patrols were sent

1918 forward and arrangements made for the regiment to work round on the left flank. It was now about 4 p.m. and the cavalry were on the Blue Line, having advanced some 14 kilometres since they had crossed what that morning were the front line trenches.

About this time General Seymour was obliged by illness to hand over his command to Lieut.-Colonel F. H. D. C. Whitmore, C.M.G., D.S.O. (commanding the 10th Royal Hussars), and Captain R. C. Gordon Canning, M.C., took over command of the 10th Royal Hussars. Captain D. E. Wallace, M.C., was Brigade Major and Captain G. Babington Staff Captain throughout these and all operations until 20th October.

At 5.30 p.m. orders were received from the Division that the 6th, 7th and Canadian Cavalry Brigades were to hold the Amiens Outer Defences (*i.e.*, the Blue Line) for the night. The 6th Cavalry Brigade took over the sector of these defences from a point East of E15 Wood to the Northern edge of Le Quesnel. " C " Battery covered the exits from Beaufort. The line consisted of a series of old trenches organised into posts, and these the Division held in conjunction with Canadian infantry. The enemy still held Le Quesnel and the high ground round it. They also occupied Beaufort and kept the valley West of E15 Wood under continual machine gun fire. The led horses were in consequence moved on to the Western slope of the valley.

Throughout the night Colonel Whitmore had to reckon with the probability of an enemy counter-attack. At 8.30 p.m. the Royals in the corner of E15 Wood were heavily shelled. The enemy on several occasions were reported to be massing and S.O.S. signals were noticed on the flanks. The night, however, passed off comparatively quietly and early on 9th August orders were received for the whole Division to concentrate along the river between Caix and Cayeux. Arrangements with regard to the relief were made direct with the Canadian infantry, who asked that the Royals and Machine Gun Squadron should remain in

position for the present in order to support an attack which was 1918
to be made at 10 a.m.   About 9 a.m. the enemy suddenly began
to shell the valley West of E15 Wood, killing a number of led
horses and inflicting considerable casualties on the men, especially
among the 3rd Dragoon Guards, who were in process of relief.
By noon the Brigade (less the Royals and Machine Gun
Squadron) was concentrated midway between Caix and Cayeux,
Brigade headquarters being in a German bath-house.   The Royals
and Machine Gun Squadron rejoined about 1.30 p.m.

At 3.40 a.m. on 10th August the Brigade received orders to
take over patrols of the 2nd Cavalry Division on the front Bouchoir
—Rouvroy, and to move forward at 5.30 a.m.   " C " Squadron
(3rd Dragoon Guards) and " A " Squadron (Royals) went on
in advance at 5 a.m. and took over these patrols, the remainder
of the Brigade moving up shortly afterwards to a point about
a mile North-west of Warvillers.   The 4th Canadian Division
and the 32nd Division were to attack at 10 a.m. and cavalry
patrols were ordered to keep in close touch.   At 10.30 a.m.,
as the infantry attack was reported to have made progress,
the 3rd Dragoon Guards and the Royals were ordered to move
up in support of their advance squadrons, the remainder of
the Brigade moving up near Beaufort.   Encouraging accounts
of the infantry advance were received, and Parvillers was
reported captured.   This information subsequently proved to
be most inaccurate.   At 12.30 Brigade headquarters moved
forward to the Warvillers—Folies road, and two officers' patrols
from the 10th Hussars were sent forward to reconnoitre the ground
for a cavalry advance.   About 1.30 p.m. Parvillers was reported
to be still strongly held by the enemy and the infantry unable
to advance.

Shortly afterwards a Company of Whippets arrived under
command of Major R. A. West, D.S.O., M.C.* (formerly a

---

* Major R. A. West was posthumously awarded the V.C. for magnificent work
which he did with the Tanks a few days later.

1918 squadron leader of the North Somerset Yeomanry) and an attack on Parvillers by the Tanks, in conjunction with the Royals and 3rd Dragoon Guards, was planned. The ground, however, was reported to be totally unsuitable for the use of cavalry. It was part of the old Somme battlefield fought over by the French in 1916, and was covered by a maze of old trenches, wire and shell holes. The Royals also reported that any advance over a country so entrenched and wired would be extremely difficult. The Tank commander, after further reconnaissance, came to the conclusion that the ground would be unsuitable even for Whippets, and the attack was therefore abandoned, the Tanks being recalled.

At 2.30 p.m. a message was received that the Canadian Cavalry Brigade was to pass through and seize the high ground North-west of Roye, and the 6th Cavalry Brigade was to be prepared to act in support. The Canadian Cavalry Brigade went forward about 5 p.m. and shortly afterwards the 10th Hussars were sent up in support. A troop of the Fort Garry Horse tried to gallop Hill 100 on the main Roye road. The ground on either side being impassable for cavalry, they were obliged to charge along the road, but never reached their objective.

At 6.15 Brigade Headquarters moved up to some old trenches just West of Le Quesnoy, and the Royals, Battery and Machine Gun Squadron closed up on the 10th Hussars one mile South-west of Le Quesnoy. The 3rd Dragoon Guards were already beyond Le Quesnoy.

Damery and Parvillers were still being obstinately held by the enemy, and orders were received that no further advance would be made that night. At 8 p.m. Brigade headquarters was heavily shelled, with casualties to the men and seven officers' chargers. One of Captain Wallace's chargers in its fright jumped clean over all four traces between the leaders and centres of a moving gun team. At 8.30 p.m. the Brigade moved back, and an hour later was concentrated West of Folies, where it bivouacked in the open fields.

Brigadier-General Ewing Paterson, D.S.O.
Commanded the 6ᵗʰ Cavalry Brigade
August 1918 - March 1919.

THE ALLIED OFFENSIVE

During the night, bombing by hostile aircraft was incessant, but fortunately there were no casualties.

Throughout the 10th the 6th C.F.A. were the furthest advanced medical unit on the Amiens—Roye road,and many infantry casualties were evacuated. After the Canadian mounted attack on Hill 100, a medical officer and bearers brought in several wounded who were reported to be still lying out.

At 5.30 p.m. on 11th August, the Brigade moved Westwards, keeping South of the main Roye road, and arrived in bivouac at Fouencamps shortly after midnight.

During these operations Lieutenant G. H. Perrett (10th Hussars) was killed, Lieutenant T. Robinson (10th Hussars) and Lieutenant A. W. G. Windham, M.C. (6th Machine Gun Squadron) were wounded. Three men were killed, 34 were wounded and 2 missing.

On 13th August the Commander-in-Chief visited Fouencamps and saw all units in the Brigade.

On 15th August Lieut.-Colonel Ewing Paterson, D.S.O. (6th Inniskilling Dragoons) assumed command of the Brigade, and the same evening the Brigade moved by night to the Le Mesge area, arriving about 4 a.m. and remained there a few days.

About midnight on 21st August the Brigade moved to the Montrelet-Fieffes area, and were in readiness to support an attack by the 4th and 6th Corps between Moyenville and Beaucourt. This was the opening of the series of battles which regained the whole of the old Somme battlefield. The Brigade remained on three hours' notice during the next three days. The heat was intense.

During the night 25th-26th the Brigade marched to Gueschart, and the following night moved to Nuncq, remaining on three hours' notice. During the next few days there were many orders and counter-orders. Finally the 10th Hussars with 4 machine guns left the Brigade area for Wailly (3 miles South of Arras). The Brigade remained on short notice.

THE ALLIED OFFENSIVE

The outstanding feature of this period was the continued advance of our troops towards the Hindenburg Line and the breaking of the Quéant-Drocourt switch by the Canadian Corps during the first few days of September (see Map 15 facing page 118). In this latter attack the 10th Hussars were to have taken part and moved up to near Arras for this purpose. They formed part of an Independent Force (under Brigadier-General R. Bruntinel, C.M.G., D.S.O.) which was divided into three groups, the leading group being commanded by Colonel Whitmore and consisting of the 10th Hussars, the Canadian Light Horse, Motor machine guns, Field artillery, and a section of the 6th Machine Gun Squadron. As soon as the Quéant-Drocourt switch had been taken, the Independent Force was to move forward, preceded by a box barrage, and seize the canal crossings at Marquion and the high ground East of the village. At zero, plus 3 hours and 20 minutes (08.20 hrs.) Colonel Whitmore's force moved off. Impassable ground on either side confined mounted troops to the road till well East of Vis-en-Artois. At 9.10 a.m. Captain the Earl of Airlie, M.C. (commanding the leading squadron of the 10th Hussars) reported that his patrols could get no further owing to machine gun fire; and that the armoured cars were unable to advance owing to strong resistance. Trench mortars were then brought into action, but with little effect. It was not until our attack developed further South that the enemy was forced to give up his position on this sector. The 10th Hussars rejoined the Brigade on 5th September.

The following day the Brigade moved to Vieil Hesdin, St. Georges, and Wail. On 16th September the Brigade moved into Hesdin preparatory to taking part in cavalry manœuvres, in which it was engaged throughout the following day, billeting the night near Doullens. On 18th September the Brigade moved back to Vieil Hesdin, and next day marched into the Rebreuve—Frévent area.

CHAPTER XIII

HONNECHY

O N 25th September the Brigade began a series of three 1918 night marches, travelling through Bus-les-Artois and Meaulte, and arriving at Hem (near Peronne) early on the 28th. On the afternoon of 29th September the Brigade marched through Peronne and Doingt to Vermand. The three regiments bivouacked in the fields along the road from Vermand to Bihucourt. There was a high wind with drenching rain all night, and there was practically no shelter of any kind.

Early that morning the 4th Army attacked the Hindenburg Line on a front of 12 miles from Holnon to Vendhuile. Opposite Bellenglise the 46th Division with life belts and rafts crossed the canal and stormed the village. Magny-la-Fosse was also taken, and the Le Tronquoy tunnel reached. To the North the 2nd American Corps, aided by the Australians, took Nauroy, Bellicourt and Guillemont Farm (see Map 9 facing page 68).

Throughout the 30th the Brigade stood-to at short notice, and on 1st October moved up to Bellenglise in readiness to go forward. Joncourt, Levergies and the Le Tronquoy tunnel had been captured that morning and a considerable breach had been made in the Hindenburg Line. Early on 3rd October the Brigade was again in assembly position South-west of Bellenglise. Le Catelet, Sequehart, Montbrehain, and Ramiecourt had been taken by the 4th Army, but the situation was not clear, and about 1 p.m. an officer's patrol under Lieutenant J. B. Bickersteth (Royals) was sent forward to gain information. It was found that our troops had been driven back out of Montbrehain, but that Ramiecourt was still in our hands. Acting on this information the Brigade moved up to Magny-la-Fosse and a little later was ordered to move forward and seize the high ground near Brancourt-

1918 le-Grand. At 4.45 p.m. the 3rd Dragoon Guards reached the Ramiecourt-Le Vergies road (near the hamlet of Preselles), the remainder of the Brigade being near Joncourt (see Map 9 facing page 68). The enemy were in strength on the high ground round Montbrehain, and the 3rd Dragoon Guards were heavily shelled. They had two men killed and 13 wounded. A number of horses were also killed. The Machine Gun Squadron and one section " C " Battery (under Lieutenant Hutchins) engaged the enemy round Montbrehain.

It was now almost dark. At 8 p.m. the 3rd Dragoon Guards (less one squadron which had been left to keep in touch with the infantry in the line) and the Royals were put at the disposal of the 46th Division, who expected a strong enemy counter-attack. Later in the evening the whole Brigade (less the advance squadron of the 3rd Dragoon Guards) concentrated North of Pontruet. Night bombing by the enemy was very severe. One bomb fell on a company of 100 or more German prisoners who happened at that moment to be only a short distance from the head of the Brigade column, and killed more than half of the party outright.

Early on 4th October the advance squadron reported that Montbrehain and adjoining high ground was still held by enemy machine guns. The Brigade remained North of Pontruet and the next day moved to Trefcon. Lieutenant H. C. Soundy (6th Innis-killing Dragoons) here joined Brigade headquarters as A.D.C.

During the following two days Montbrehain and Beaurevoir were captured and the enemy forced to withdraw from the Hindenburg Line at La Terrière and to the North.

On the 8th October the 3rd and 4th Armies attacked on a front which extended from Sequehart to the South of Cambrai. At 3.45 a.m. that morning the Brigade marched from Trefcon to a concentration area near Magny-la-Fosse (see Map 9 facing page 68). From 10 a.m. till noon the Brigade moved by successive bounds to the valley 2,000 yards North-east of

Estrées. Our infantry were then in and beyond Serain and   1918
Prémont, and several regiments of the 1st Cavalry Division
were also engaged. About dusk the Brigade moved back to
near Magny-la-Fosse. Brigade headquarters was established in
a room in the famous Hindenburg Tunnel, which links up Bellicourt, Nauroy, Magny-la-Fosse and Le Tronquoy by a vast
subterranean system. The tunnel, which resembled a large under-
ground town, was provided with a light railway (with sidings) and
was lit by electricity throughout. The four Germans who
managed the two electric light plants were captured at the same time
as the tunnel and were obliged to continue working for the British.
They pretended for several days that one of the electric plants was
mined, but on the engine being started up in the presence of one
British officer (the tunnel having first been cleared of all troops for
safety) this proved to be false.

Night bombing by the enemy was again very severe. No
fires could be lighted after dark and throughout these operations
it was impossible to arrange for the men to have any hot meals either
when starting before dawn or on arrival in bivouac after sundown.
Infantry " cookers " would have been invaluable.

At 1.50 a.m. on 9th October, orders were received for the
Brigade to concentrate by 7 a.m. near Genève. This entailed
moving in the dark over country covered with wire and trenches.
On arriving at Genève General Paterson and Captain Wallace went
on to a conference at advanced divisional Headquarters, and at
8.35 a.m. the Brigade was ordered to move forward at the
trot, as our infantry were reported East of Maretz and touch
had been lost with the enemy. The Royals acted as advance
guard to the Brigade and were ordered to move immediately,
keeping parallel to and South of the main Le Cateau road, the
10th Hussars to follow the Royals with one squadron as right flank
guard. The Canadian Cavalry Brigade was on the left. The
Brigade moved at a fast pace to Maretz, and there came under fire

1918   from the direction of Honnechy and Escaufourt.   " C " Squadron (Royals) (Captain W. P. Browne, M.C.) was ordered to push on if possible towards Honnechy and Maurois.   This squadron reached the quarry near the railway on the Western outskirts of Honnechy.   Lieutenant J. F. Houstoun-Boswall with his scouts pushed forward to a house in the railway fork South-west of the village.   The enemy were occupying the hedges and orchards on the edge of Honnechy, and also the high ground to the South.

While making a personal reconnaissance about 11.30 a.m., General Paterson met the Brigade Major of the Infantry Brigade which had advanced East of Maretz and was now being held up by the enemy in and around Honnechy.   The latter said that the infantry were exhausted and that in view of the strong forces opposed to them it was not intended to advance further that day. About noon a conference was held between Major-General Harman commanding the 3rd Cavalry Division, and the G.Os.C. 6th and Canadian Cavalry Brigades.   It appeared that the Canadian Cavalry Brigade was held up and could not advance further, unless Honnechy and Reumont were captured.   It was therefore decided that the 6th Cavalry Brigade should take these villages as soon as possible, and then seize the high ground West of Le Cateau.   The Inniskilling Dragoons from the 7th Cavalry Brigade were placed at the disposal of General Paterson and orders were issued for the attack to take place at 2 p.m.

The general idea of the operations was that the Royals should make a mounted attack on Honnechy and Maurois from the West and from the positions already held by that regiment.   The 10th Hussars were to follow in support of the Royals and advance as the attack progressed.   The 3rd Dragoon Guards were to advance from the North of Busigny and attack Honnechy from the South-west. The Inniskilling Dragoons were to follow in support of the 3rd Dragoon Guards and form a defensive flank facing Escaufourt and Bois Proyart.   " C " Battery was to take up a position South-east of

Maretz and fire on the South-western outskirts of Honnechy, while 1918 our troops were advancing. The 6th Machine Gun Squadron was to cover the advance of the Royals and 3rd Dragoon Guards and keep down the enemy's fire from Honnechy.

The attack of the Royals and 3rd Dragoon Guards began simultaneously. As each unit advanced heavy H.E. and machine gun fire was opened on them. A large number of enemy aircraft also suddenly appeared and coming down to a low altitude followed the attacking troops with bombs and machine gun fire.

The Royals almost at once came to a deep railway cutting which was not marked on the map and had to swing northwards, cross the railway further up and gallop round the northern edge of Maurois. They arrived at a farm on the Le Cateau road midway between Maurois and Reumont. Reumont was still held and enemy machine guns were firing straight down the road from the village at a range of about 400 yards. Captain Browne's Squadron, which was still leading, suffered some casualties in trying to cross. Colonel Wormald decided to get his regiment across the road slightly further back and then seize the high ground South-east of Reumont. This operation was carried out with signal success, and the Royals gained the ridge, forcing the enemy to retire out of Reumont.

Meanwhile, the 3rd Dragoon Guards advanced from North of Busigny. Captain N. K. Worthington's Squadron which was leading at once came under heavy enfilade fire from the direction of Escaufourt and Bois Proyart. The going was fairly good but the ground was cut up by numerous small ditches. There was one wide brook with a bad take-off, but not a single horse refused. Fortunately the ground was free of wire. As each squadron came to the railway embankment it had to close in to pass under the bridge by which the railway crossed the road. It was here that most of the casualties occurred. The squadrons then opened out again and made the final gallop towards Honnechy (which was taken about 2.30 p.m.) afterwards occupying the orchards to the East of

1918 the village. The orchards were soon heavily shelled, and Colonel Rome was wounded.

This mounted attack by the Royals and 3rd Dragoon Guards was carried out with great dash and skill. The bursting H.E., the rattle of the machine gun fire both from the ground and from the air, the explosion of the bombs dropped from the aeroplanes—all contributed to make the noise absolutely deafening.

As the two regiments advanced through the infantry the latter rose as one man and advanced with a great cheer, forgetting their former weariness and following in close support. This successful attack enabled the Canadian Cavalry Brigade on the North of the Le Cateau road to advance and capture several hundred prisoners, about seventy machine guns, and several guns and trench mortars.

Enemy fire had now increased in volume, and Honnechy and all positions held by the Brigade were under continuous shelling. The Brigade suffered considerable casualties both in men and horses, especially the 3rd Dragoon Guards, who had also lost heavily during their advance. From the position gained considerable forces of the enemy, with a line of machine guns backed by several field guns, could be seen occupying the ridge which just hid Le Cateau from view. At this time the only troops in hand were one squadron of the 10th Hussars holding the Eastern edge of Honnechy, and half the Machine Gun Squadron who were with them. At 5 p.m. verbal orders were given to Colonel Wormald and Colonel Whitmore to push on as soon as possible. A few minutes later, however, orders were received from the 3rd Cavalry Division that the 7th Cavalry Brigade was to seize the final objective, the 6th Cavalry Brigade remaining in close support. The Inniskillings who had been ordered to push on towards Le Cateau were therefore diverted to the 7th Cavalry Brigade, less one squadron, which remained on the right flank.

A line of posts and machine guns was then established from Honnechy to Reumont, both inclusive. Heavy machine gun fire

HONNECHY

continued from East of Reumont, and there was considerable shelling with H.E. and Blue Cross. A low-flying aeroplane succeeded in dropping two bombs on a squadron of the 10th Hussars and on a troop of the Royals, which wounded four officers. The same bombs killed and wounded a number of men and killed many horses. Brigade headquarters was established in the farm on the Le Cateau road between Reumont and Maurois. The 6th C.F.A. opened a large dressing station at Maretz during the afternoon, where many sick and wounded civilians were treated and fed as well as the ordinary casualties.

Meanwhile the Canadian Cavalry Brigade on the left had reached Troisvilles and the high ground to the East of it with one squadron at Rambourlieux Farm, the 7th Cavalry Brigade being in touch with them to the South. It was now dark and no further progress could be made. The 18th Corps Cyclists came up and took over the outpost line, the Royals then being in support, and the 3rd Dragoon Guards, 10th Hussars, and 7th Dragoon Guards in reserve. Except for intermittent shelling, the night passed quietly.

At 5 a.m. on 10th October, the Brigade concentrated in the valley between Reumont and Troisvilles and got into touch with 7th Cavalry Brigade, who were near Rambourlieux Farm. At 8 a.m. the Brigade moved up to the East of Troisvilles in closer support, moving back in the early afternoon to its former position to make room for the 7th Cavalry Brigade, who were being shelled. " C " Battery R.H.A. came under orders of C.R.H.A., and took part in the barrage during the infantry attack at 5 p.m., rejoining in the evening. One direct hit mortally wounded Lieutenant B. McLachlan, M.C., killed two men, wounded three, and damaged 14 wheels so badly that they were unfit for further use. During the afternoon the Brigade moved back to Montigny and went into bivouac outside the village. On 11th October the Brigade moved to Elincourt, where all men and horses were under cover.

1918   The casualties were:—3rd Dragoon Guards: Lieutenant V. Oakley-Brown (killed), Lieutenant E. A. L. Kittle (died of wounds), Lieut.-Colonel C. L. Rome, D.S.O., Captain H. P. Holt, Lieutenant B. H. Osmaston (wounded); other ranks, 2 killed, 27 wounded. The Royal Dragoons: Other ranks, 4 killed, 29 wounded. 10th Hussars: Captain W. S. Murland, Lieutenant F. C. Drake, M.C., Lieutenant S. A. Ralli, Lieutenant S. J. Tufnell (Essex Yeomanry, attached 10th Hussars), Lieutenant W. Ritchie (Essex Yeomanry, attached 10th Hussars) wounded; other ranks, 7 killed. "C" Battery R.H.A.: Lieutenant B. McLachlan, M.C. (killed), Lieutenant A. Bontor (wounded); other ranks, 1 killed, 4 wounded. 6th Machine Gun Squadron: Lieutenant H. N. Ellis (killed); other ranks, 3 killed.   The 3rd Dragoon Guards lost 90 horses, the Royals 34, and the 10th Hussars 106.

On 13th October the Brigade marched across country to Banteux on the canal De l'Escaut.   The village was totally destroyed and all ranks were in the open.   The following day the Brigade marched to Hennois Wood, Manancourt and Etricourt.   The men were in huts and all horses picketed out.   The desolation of this devastated area was appalling.   Hardly a house was standing in any of the villages and the land was covered with rank grass and cut up by endless trenches and belts of rusty wire.

By a curious chance the grave of Captain C. R. Tidswell (Royals), who had left the regiment in 1915 to join the R.F.C. and had been missing for many months, was found clearly marked on the hillside near the huts occupied by his old regiment.

During the next few days the Brigade was occupied in re-fitting, and mounted reinforcements arrived.

The Germans continued to retreat steadily along the whole front.   Ostend, Lille and Douai fell in one day.

On 20th October Captain E. A. Fielden, M.C., returned from Cambridge and again assumed the duties of Brigade Major, Captain D. E. Wallace, M.C., becoming Staff Captain.

CHAPTER XIV.

THE ARMISTICE

O N 6th November the Brigade marched through Havrin- 1918
court to Marquion, and the following day to Esquerchin
(2 miles West of Douai). Heavy rain fell throughout
these two days. On 8th November the march was
continued to Peronne—Louvil—Fretin (about 6 miles
South-east of Lille).

That morning our troops had occupied the Western part of
Tournai and had crossed the Scheldt South of Antoing. On
9th November the Germans were retreating along the whole front
of the five British armies.

On 10th November the Brigade marched to Bachy, and later
in the morning crossed the Belgian frontier and reached Rumes
about 4 miles South-west of Tournai. It was here that news of
the German Emperor's flight to Holland was first received. At
3 p.m. the Brigade marched through the Southern outskirts of
Tournai, crossed the Scheldt at Vaulx-le-Tournai, and stayed the
night at Gaurain-Ramcroix.

At 6 a.m. on 11th November, General Paterson and Captain
Fielden attended a conference at Divisional headquarters at Antoing,
and at 8.15 a.m. the Brigade concentrated at the 11th mile-
stone on the Tournai—Leuze road. A quarter of an hour later the
Brigade moved forward as advance guard to the 3rd Cavalry
Division with objective Enghien—Steenkerque. The Royals were
in front as advance guard to the Brigade with the line Ath—Chièvres
as first objective. The 10th Hussars who were patrolling towards
Enghien and Steenkerque were in contact with the enemy about
11.30 a.m. North of Silly, and it is certain that the whole Brigade
would have been in action by noon.

About 10 a.m. the head of the main body had just reached the
centre of the town of Leuze, when it was overtaken by a cavalry

1918 corps car, in which was a staff officer, who handed the following official telegram to General Paterson :—

TO { 1st Cav Div
     3rd Cav Div

GC 303   11

Hostilities will cease at 11 00 today Nov 11 aaa troops will stand fast on position reached at hour named aaa line of outposts will be established and reported to Corps HQ aaa remainder of troops will be collected and organised ready to meet any demand aaa all military precautions will be preserved and there will be no communication with enemy aaa further instructions will be issued aaa acknowledge

FROM   Cav Corps

PLACE

TIME   08.10   G. Reynolds, Major

The Brigade dismounted and messages were at once sent to the Royals and to all patrols repeating this telegram and ordering them to stand fast where they were. At 11 a.m. the actual hour when hostilities ceased, an impromptu ceremony took place in the market square of Leuze. An infantry battalion (a London Regiment) with its band happened to be there. Mounted men were summoned from each of the units present with the Brigade, and these formed three sides of a square, the infantry the fourth. In the centre of the square were the Mayor of Leuze, the G.O.C. 6th Cavalry Brigade, the band and the regimental trumpeters. The market place was full of civilians, and every window and door was crowded. As the last stroke of 11.0 died away, the trumpeters sounded " Stand Fast " and " Cease Fire," and then as the infantry

THE ARMISTICE

presented arms, the band played "God Save the King," followed by the Belgian and French national anthems. It was a memorable and intensely moving scene.

The Brigade remained on the outskirts of Leuze till the afternoon, and then marched back to Gaurain Ramcroix, moving the following day about three miles South-east to the Ponenche area.

The next four days were spent in a thorough clean-up. One squadron (10th Hussars) joined Headquarters Cavalry Corps as escort to the Corps Commander, and one troop (3rd Dragoon Guards) joined Headquarters 3rd Cavalry Division as escort to Major General A. E. W. Harman, D.S.O.

Maps were now issued showing the Zones allotted to the Allied Armies in their advance through Belgium into Germany and marking the various Lines which must be free of all German troops by a certain date.

THE BREAK-UP OF THE BRIGADE

1918 O N 17th November, in accordance with the terms of the Armistice, the Brigade began its march Eastwards into Belgium. All bridges and important cross roads as well as miles of railway track were found prepared for demolition, and the Field Troop R.E. which was attached to the Brigade during the march was kept busy. The first night was spent in an area about 3 miles West of Enghien. The Royals held a line of outposts immediately on the outskirts of the town.

  The main road from Leuze to Enghien presented a most extraordinary sight. Literally thousands of Belgian and French civilians, who had been deported from their homes by the Germans and were now at last set free, were making their way westwards on foot. The hand-carts and barrows on which they carried their few belongings were covered with the flags of the Allies. Every now and again the people, tired but happy, stopped and cheered the troops. Among the civilians were scores of liberated British prisoners. They were dressed in such an assortment of ragged garments that it was difficult to recognise them. Many were ill and nearly all of them were hungry. A system was devised by which motor ambulances moving with the mounted troops carried extra rations, and the men were properly fed and passed back from one headquarters to another.

  On 18th November the Brigade marched through Enghien and was billeted at Saintes, Tubise, Quenast. On 20th November, at the request of the Burgermestre for assistance, one troop (Royals) was sent forward to Hal to quell disturbances. The civilian population had been mobbing persons who were considered guilty of pro-German sympathies during the enemy occupation.

THE BREAK-UP OF THE BRIGADE

On 21st November the Brigade marched across the field of
Waterloo.

On this very ground over one hundred years before The Royal
Dragoons had taken part in the famous charge of the Union Brigade.
They were then brigaded under General Sir William Ponsonby with
the 2nd Dragoons (Royal Scots Greys) and the 6th (Inniskilling)
Dragoons. At about 1.30 p.m. on 18th June, 1815, D'Erlon's
brigade of 20,000 men had made an overwhelming attack, as a result
of which a Belgian brigade had been completely scattered, the
supporting British infantry broken, and many guns captured. The
whole Allied position was thus endangered, and at this critical
moment the Union Brigade was ordered to charge. The three
regiments deployed into line, halted to allow the broken infantry
to retire through them, and swept forward in an irresistible charge.
The French columns were dispersed in all directions. " Every-
" where the Royals, Greys and Inniskillings were to be seen
" trampling down and sabring the fugitives."

The night of 21st November the Brigade billeted in the area
round Ottignies, moving on the following day to Eghezée. Both
here and in the Ottignies area guards were left to take over German
material which had been left in accordance with the Armistice terms.
The following material was found in Ottignies station and sidings
alone :—22 locomotives, 38 passenger coaches, 390 trucks containing ammunition, coal and wood, 76 empty trucks, 5 new aeroplanes
packed on trucks. At Eghezée on the 23rd November over
50 guns of all calibres and many trench mortars were handed over
personally by a German officer to Brigade headquarters.

In every village and town throughout the advance the Brigade
was received with the greatest enthusiasm by the Belgian population.
Their genuine pleasure at the sight of British troops after four
years of German occupation was shown by the crowds of cheering
people who lined the roads, by the triumphal arches, bands, speeches

THE BREAK-UP OF THE BRIGADE

1918 and official receptions, and by an intense desire to do everything to make the troops comfortable.

On 24th November "A" Squadron (Royals) (Captain E. W. T. Miles, M.C.) marched to Namur and took over guards from the 11th Hussars, one troop being billeted on the top of the citadel.   The same day the Brigade moved a few miles South, Brigade headquarters being at Upigny.   The Royals were billeted a few miles from Namur near three enormous Zeppelin hangars, from which several of the air raids on London had started during the earlier part of the war.

Owing to the great difficulties of transport only the 2nd Army (to which was attached the 1st Cavalry Division) advanced into Germany.   The 4th Army (to which the 2nd and 3rd Cavalry Divisions were attached) remained in Belgium.   The Brigade remained in the Upigny area until 12th December, when it marched eastwards and staying one night in the neighbourhood of Vinalmont moved the following day into permanent winter billets about ten miles West of Liége.

Brigade Headquarters (including the 6th Signal Troop and the 13th M.V.S.) were at Stockay, the 3rd Dragoon Guards at St. Georges, The Royal Dragoons at Jehay, the 10th Royal Hussars at Seraing-le-Chateau, "C" Battery R.H.A. at Awirs, the 6th Machine Gun Squadron at Amay, the 6th C.F.A. at La Mallieue.

1919   In the latter part of December demobilisation began, and during the month of January proceeded at the average rate of 2 officers and 40 other ranks a day.

At the end of January all horses were classified, and during February "C" and "Y" horses were sent to England and "Z" horses were disposed of at local sales at Liége and Huy.   Only "X" horses, which were those selected for the Army of Occupation and officers' chargers, remained.   Meanwhile, demobilisation continued fairly steadily, till there were only just sufficient men left to look after the horses.

THE BREAK-UP OF THE BRIGADE

Units now began to make preparations to leave the Brigade for their various destinations, and on the departure of each regiment those who still remained turned out to wish the officers and men who were leaving farewell and good luck.

On 7th March the 3rd Dragoon Guards (Lieut.-Colonel C. L. Rome, D.S.O.) which had been reduced to Cadre " A " strength, proceeded by lorry to the cadre area near Verviers. A few weeks later they returned to Tidworth, preparatory to going abroad the following autumn.

A few days later it was definitely decided that the Royals and the 10th Hussars were to form part of the Army of the Rhine.

On 14th March the 10th Royal Hussars (Lieut.-Colonel F. H. D. C. Whitmore, C.M.G., D.S.O.) started on their march into Germany.

Meanwhile " C " Battery R.H.A. (Major D. Scott, M.C.) had already been reduced to Cadre "A" strength, and was now under orders of C.R.H.A. awaiting transportation to England. The 6th Machine Gun Squadron (Major J. C. Humfrey, M.C.) was in process of being broken up, all retainable men being sent to machine gun squadrons in Germany. The 6th C.F.A. (Lieut.-Colonel C. H. Stringer, D.S.O.) was being reduced to cadre under the orders of the A.D.M.S., and the 6th Signal Troop and the 13th M.V.S. were also being gradually brought down to minimum strength.

On 18th March The Royal Dragoons (Lieut.-Colonel F. W. Wormald, D.S.O.) left the area and began a trek of several days to Cologne.

General Paterson issued a Special Order of the Day to each unit before it left the Brigade, thanking officers, N.C.O.s and men for their splendid work and wishing them good luck. In the course of a letter given to those men who were returning to civil life, he wrote : " You have the satisfaction of knowing that you " have served your country well and that whatever your military rank " and standing may have been, your efforts have really helped to

THE BREAK-UP OF THE BRIGADE

1919 " bring about the defeat of the Germans.   As a civilian you will
" find yourself confronted by many perplexing problems.   Keep a
" level head and play the game in peace as admirably as you have
" played it in war."

Finally, Brigade headquarters itself, which no longer had any
troops to administer, was reduced to cadre.   Captain Wallace had
already left the Brigade and General Paterson and his A.D.C. now
returned to England.   The only officers who remained for a time
were Captain E. A. Fielden, M.C. (10th Hussars) and Captain C. J.
Tindell-Green (R.A.S.C.).

By 20th March, 1919, the 6th Cavalry Brigade had ceased
to exist.

Few who had been with the Brigade any length of time
witnessed its complete dispersal without regret.   The relief that
hostilities had ceased did not detract from the feeling of genuine
sorrow that the time had come for many good friends to part.   In the
vicissitudes of four and a half years of war men learn to know and
value each other, and many friendships are formed.   With the prospect of peace came a more vivid understanding how great was the
sacrifice of those countless friends who would never return.   As unit
after unit left the Brigade for their various destinations, there were
many, both officers and men, who realised that a memorable chapter
in their lives had at last drawn to a close.   But whatever the personal
feelings of each might be, there was satisfaction in knowing that the
6th Cavalry Brigade (from the day of its formation on Salisbury
Plain in 1914 to the day of its final break-up in the neighbourhood
of Liége in 1919) had not only played a part worthy of the famous
regiments which had served in it, but had also under conditions which
called for patience, adaptability and courage upheld the highest
traditions of the British Cavalry.